Island Adventure
Workbook for Books

Notes on the Island Adventure Series

Island Adventure Series

Introduction
The Island Adventure Series is aimed at older pupils who need to learn the Phonic Code in order to make progress in their reading. The books introduce the vowel sounds and their alternative spellings. The series includes 10 books, each with a phonic focus.
This workbook, based on the stories, includes a variety of activities which teach and consolidate an understanding of the Phonic Code.

Pronunciation
At the beginning of each book, there is a word list to help the reader learn the alternative spellings of vowel sounds in the English Phonic Code. Pronunciation of some sounds may vary, according to regional accents. The word lists may not always match the pronunciation of the pupil. This point should be discussed and the lists adapted to the pupil.

Blending not guessing
Pupils should be encouraged to blend the sounds into words. If there are spellings they do not know, point to the part of the word that is new and tell them the sound. Then get the pupil to blend the sounds into the word.

Use precise pronunciation
When blending sounds together, say the consonants without the added 'uh' sound.
e.g. 'c' 'a' 't' not 'cuh' 'a' 'tuh'.

Teaching alternative spellings
The English Phonic Code is complex. This series presents 5–7 alternative spellings for a vowel sound. The teacher may need to introduce these spellings gradually if the pupil has difficulty learning all the alternative spellings at a time.

Splitting multisyllabic words
At the bottom of every page, a few multisyllabic words are split for the reader. This will enable the reader to tackle longer words independently. There are a number of ways to split multisyllabic words. The approach taken, in this series, is to split the word in the most 'reader–friendly' way.

New vocabulary
Each new book offers an opportunity to learn new vocabulary on the 'vocabulary page'. This page explains the words as they appear in the context of the text. The teacher may wish to discuss additional meanings of the word with the pupil.

The workbook

The workbook complements the Island Adventure Series. The 10 chapters in the workbook correlate to the 10 books in the series. Each chapter offers activities based on the phonic focus of each of the books. Before reading the books, pupils would benefit from practising word building, blending, reading and sorting activities. These activities feature at the beginning of every chapter. Follow-up activities, such as comprehension, spelling and various games, should be used after reading the texts. The teacher can select from the activities in each chapter to maintain interest and variety.

An instruction for every activity in the workbook appears at the bottom of each page.

Phonic sequence in the Island Adventure Series: Books 1–10

Book	Title	Phoneme focus	Spellings
1	Saving the Day	'ae'	ay, ai, a, a-e, ea, ey
2	Sea Change	'ee'	ee, ea, e, y, e-e, ie, ei
3	Coast to Coast	'oe'	ow, oa, o, oe, o-e,
4	A World Away	'er'	er, ir, ur, or, ear
5	Sounds and Shadows	'ow' and 'oi'	ow, ou & oy, oi
6	A Shrewd Route	'oo'	oo, ue, u-e, ew, ou, u
7	An Amazing Find	'ie'	igh, ie, i-e, i, y
8	Awesome Morning	'or'	or, ore, a, aw, awe, au, ar, al, ough
9	Don't be Scared	'air'	air, are, ear, ere, eir
10	Arty Party	'ar'	ar, a, al, ear au,

Island Adventure Series
Activity Book

for Books 1–10

Name: ______________________________

Island Adventure Series
Book 1: Saving the Day

Contents

Book 1
Blending and segmenting: 'ae'

rain | r | ai | n

they

gate | | a | | e

baby

great

train

plate

spray

snake

afraid

breaking

fainted

payment

Blend the sounds into a word. Segment the word into sounds by writing one sound in each square.
Split vowel spellings (a–e) are represented by half squares linked together.

Book 1
Reading and sorting words with 'ae' spellings

ea	ai	ay	a	a–e	ey

strain	blame	great	brain
train	able	say	faint
steak	late	lazy	they
nail	display	flame	angel
day	pain	break	mate
prey	stay	trail	grapes
making	drain	whale	spray
stain	frame	baby	Book 1 Reading cards 'ae' spellings

Photocopy this page onto card and cut into reading cards.
Store cards in an envelope and stick the label on the front for reference.
Can also be photocopied twice on different coloured card and cut into cards to
make a simple matching game.

Book 1

Reading and spelling words with 'ae' spellings

ai	ay	a-e
_______	_______	_______
_______	_______	_______
_______	_______	_______
_______	_______	_______

a	ea	ey
_______	_______	_______
_______	_______	_______
_______	_______	

> sale rain David great May late tray they
> flame day chain spray blame steak pain
> table fail fade baby break prey

List the words according to the 'ae' spellings.

Book 1

Timed reading of words with 'ae' spellings

sale   able   May   faint   great   shame   late
paint   tray   nail   sacred   flame   quaint   cupcake
day   pain   table   mate   stay   trail   haze
making   drain   whale   spray   strain   blame
brain   stain   they   fade   clay   Spain   break

1st try   Time:

---

sale   able   May   faint   great   shame   late
paint   tray   nail   sacred   flame   quaint   cupcake
day   pain   table   mate   stay   trail   haze
making   drain   whale   spray   strain   blame
brain   stain   they   fade   clay   Spain   break

2nd try   Time:

---

sale   able   May   faint   great   shame   late
paint   tray   nail   sacred   flame   quaint   cupcake
day   pain   table   mate   stay   trail   haze
making   drain   whale   spray   strain   blame
brain   stain   they   fade   clay   Spain   break

3rd try   Time:

This timed reading exercise is for the pupil to improve his/her reading speed and fluency. Ask the pupil to read the words as fast as he/she can. Record the time in the box. Repeat the exercise. This sheet can be cut or folded along the dotted lines to allow for different presentations.

Book 1

Chunking two-syllable words with 'ae'

gatecrash	gate	crash	gatecrash
haystack			
payment			
complain			
cupcake			
table			
blameless			
railway			
display			
escape			
greatness			
afraid			
awake			
making			

Split the word into two syllables. Write each syllable in a box.
Write the whole word while saying the syllables.

Book 1

Phonic patterns

Colour in the words with 'ae' spellings.

understand	trail	break	nailbrush
shame	rubber	flute	black
making	rattle	complain	fade
landing	they	explain	band
dismay	great	table	delay

Fold this sheet on the dotted line. Read the words in the column on the left. Listen to the sounds in the words. Colour in the lozenges with words that have 'ae' spellings. Repeat this in the other columns. Unfold the sheet and check the correct words have been coloured in.

Is it true?

Jack and Snub are staying with Gran and
Grandpa. Grandpa has a fat cat called
Skiffle. Snub makes a sketch in the sand
with a stick. It is a sketch of a fish. Jack
gets lost and falls into a blanket bog. Gran
has made them a cake with lots of plums
in it. The wind and the rain smash up
Grandpa's boat.

There are **5** things in the story above that are
not true. Can you spot them?

Ask the pupil to read the text carefully and circle any false information
that has been planted in the story.

Book 1

Picture the scene

There is a cliff behind Jack.

Gran's workshop is on the top of the cliff.

Jack is standing on a beach made of pebbles and sand.

There are three birds flying in the sky above the cliff.

The sun is in the sky, on the left-hand side of the picture.

Ask the pupil to read the text carefully and draw the details of the picture as described in the text.
Encourage them to read through all the text carefully before they begin working so they can plan their drawing.
This sheet may be photocopied by the purchaser. © Phonic Books Ltd 2019

Book 1

Dictation

"Got it!" said Gran, with a big grin. Jack grinned too. It was a

__ __ ___ __ shot. "That was a long __ ___ __   __ __ __ ___,"

said Gran.

"It's __ __ __ ___ __   __ long __ ___ __ with your job," said

Jack. "I'll __ __ __ __ you back to Snub."

Jack's little sister, Snub, was __ __ ___ __ ___ on the beach

with Grandpa and his dog, Skiffle.

The __ __ ___ __ __ __ Snub __ __ __ __ from Gran and

had stuck. Snub was scratching __ ___ __ __ in the damp

sand with a stick. "It looks __ __ ___ __, Snub!" said Jack.

"Got it!" said Gran, with a big grin. Jack grinned too. It was a **g r ea t** shot. "That was a long **w ai t t o d ay**," said Gran.

"It's **a l w ay s a** long **w ai t** with your job," said Jack. "I'll **r a c e** you back to Snub."

Jack's little sister, Snub, was **p l ay i ng** on the beach with Grandpa and his dog, Skiffle.

The **n i ck n a m e** Snub **c a m e** from Gran and had stuck. Snub was scratching **a sh a p e** in the damp sand with a stick. "It looks **g r ea t**, Snub!" said Jack.

Use the text at the bottom of the page for dictation. The section for dictation can either be cut off by the teacher or folded along the dotted line to allow the pupil to self-check their spellings on completion.
Dictate the passage to the pupil. Ask them to spell the missing words, writing a sound on each line.
Explain that a longer line indicates a spelling with more than one letter e.g. <u>r</u> <u>ai</u> <u>n</u>.

Book 1

Punctuation exercise

Capital letters and full stops

it had rained for days and days it was great to see the sun again jack gazed across at the workshop grandpa had made for gran at the top of the cliff it clung to the edge of the land like a limpet a sudden wail from gran gave jack a shock

There are **9** capital letters and **5** full stops missing.

Did you spot them all?

Ask the pupil to read through the text and add in capital letters and full stops where necessary.
Encourage the pupil to read aloud as this will help him/her identify where the sentences stop.

Book 1

Developing vocabulary: **scanned**

The word 'scanned' is used here in Book 1:

'Scanned' is another word for looking. It is used when you are peering or looking at something.

Circle the word or phrase that could be replaced with the word 'scanned' in the following text:

The sun lit up the sky like golden flames as the sun set into the sea. The old man looked at the waves, looking for seals.

Can you write two different sentences of your own using the word 'scanned'?

1.

____

____

2.

____

____

Book 1

Character profile

Use the word bank to help you describe Snub.

making things   cheese on toast   playing   animal lover

having fun   sleeping   sister   running

skipping

Name _______________

Age _______________

Loves ____

Hates _Snub hates having to go to bed!_
____

Hobbies ____

Favourite food ____

This is a writing frame to help structure creative writing. Ask the pupil to use words from the word bank to help them create a character profile for Snub. They will know some things from the story, but encourage them to be creative in their answers and to try to write in full sentences, using capital letters and full stops. This framework can also be used as a planning document for a piece of free writing.

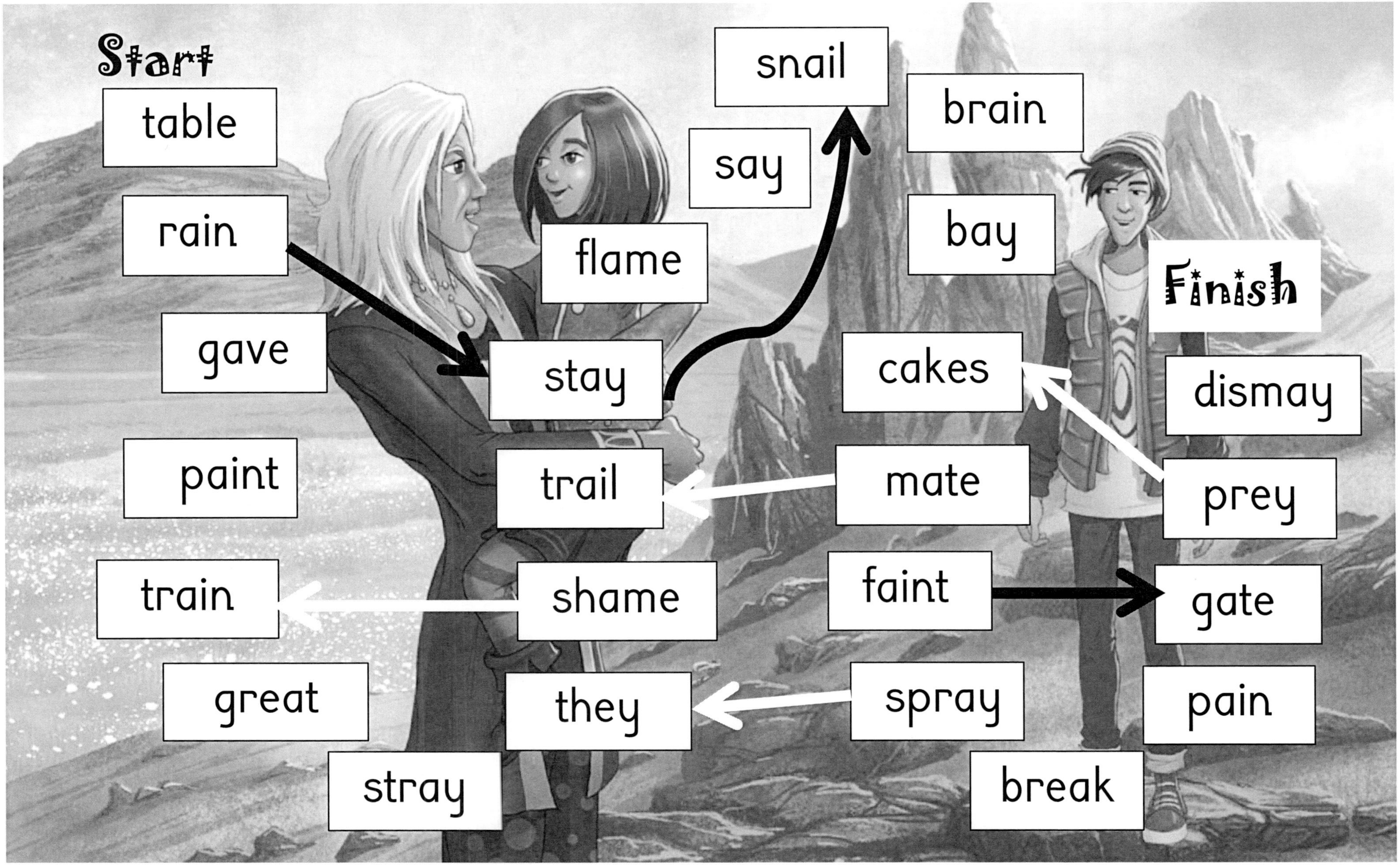

A game for 1–4 players: Play with counters and dice.
Players should read aloud the words that they land on at the end of each turn and follow the black and white direction arrows if they land on them.

This sheet may be photocopied by the purchaser. © Phonic Books Ltd 2019

Book 1

Non fiction:

Blanket bogs – Safety leaflet

Bogs are made up of a dark, wet soil known as peat. Peat is made up of dead plant material, often mosses. Bogs are often home to a number of rare plant and animal species. Rare animals include the otter and some birds of prey. Bogs often have grass, moss and plants growing on them and look like normal land. In fact they are very watery and can be as much as 90% water and only 10% solid material. This can make them very dangerous for walkers. The word 'bog' comes from the Irish word 'bogach' meaning soft.

The world's largest peat bog is called the Congo and it is as big as England!

Walkers need to know how to cross a bog safely. Rain can make the top layers of the bog soak up water like a sponge. Snow can conceal deep puddles. It is generally safer to visit bogs in dry weather. It is always sensible to travel with someone else and not on your own and to carry a mobile phone. Puddles can be very deceptive and what looks like a small puddle or a narrow stream could be very deep. If a walker does accidentally fall into a bog they must try not to panic as this could make things worse. Grabbing onto a stick or something nearby can be helpful and be a means of climbing out. Rescuers can also help by offering a scarf or belt to hang onto. It is important the rescuer makes sure they are on safe ground before trying to help.

If a walker is sunk into a bog up to waist level they should try to calmly release one leg at a time. They should then lean backwards to distribute their weight evenly over the surface of the bog. Once both legs are free they can slowly crawl to more solid ground.

Blanket bogs: information for walkers

This sheet provides the information needed to make a safety leaflet. Ask the pupil to read the text carefully and circle the information they will need to make their flyer. Explain that they need to look for information that will be relevant. They can then use this information to create the flyer in the box below.

Book 1

Dice game: words with 'ae' spellings

⚀	⚁	⚂	⚃	⚄	⚅
stay	gate	nail	acorn	tray	great
table	they	late	waist	break	spray
game	trail	cable	cake	David	say
brain	baby	steak	same	aim	able
trail	tape	make	day	blame	wait

This game is for two players. Each player needs a batch of counters of one colour. The players take turns to throw the die. They read a word in the column that corresponds to the number on the die and place their counter on that word. The first to have three of his/her counters in a row in any direction is the winner.

This sheet may be photocopied by the purchaser.   © Phonic Books Ltd 2019

Book 1

Spelling assessment for words with 'ae' spellings

1.

ai	**ay**	**a**	**a–e**	**ea**	**ey**
rain	day	baby	name	break	they
faint	play	table	late	steak	prey
brain	spray	bacon	shame	great	

2.

ai	**ay**	**a**	**a–e**	**ea**
sprain	payment	David	gatecrash	breaking
fainted	today	acorn	blameless	steakhouse
explain	haystack	making		

These lists can be used as a spelling assessment at the end of each book. The teacher can add words from list 2 for pupils who are ready for that stage. When dictating a word, first say the word on its own. Next, say a sentence with the word in it (to put the word in the context of a sentence) and then repeat the word. This ensures that the pupil has heard the word correctly, e.g. "Fainted. The boy fainted when he saw the mouse. Fainted."

Island Adventure Series
Book 2: Sea Change

Contents

Book 2: Blending and segmenting: 'ee'

feel	f	ee	l		
each					
theme		e		e	
she					
grief					
baby					
delete						
sheep					
dream					
shield					
angry					
began					
seizing					

Blend the sounds into a word. Segment the word into sounds by writing one sound in each square.
Split vowel spellings (e–e) are represented by half squares linked together.
This sheet may be photocopied by the purchaser. © Phonic Books Ltd 2019

Book 2: Reading and sorting words with 'ee' spellings

ee	ea	e	ie	ei	e–e	y

reed	seem	she	field
seize	Pete	sunny	messy
creep	sneak	belong	shield
receive	delete	relax	agree
stream	grief	complete	ceiling
indeed	frilly	release	repeat
recede	shriek	begin	scream
feeling	steal	compete	thief

Photocopy this page onto card and cut out the words. Read and sort the cards out
according to the 'ee' headings at the top of the page.
This sheet may be photocopied by the purchaser. © Phonic Books Ltd 2019

Reading and spelling words with 'ee' spellings

Boxes with 'ee' spellings, each with blank lines:

ee
______
______
______
______

ea
______
______
______
______

e
______
______

ei
______
______

y
______
______

ie
______
______

e-e
______
______

need   shriek   reach   Pete   me   quickly   green   grieve
sneak   empty   conceive   safety   sweet   beach   grief
seize   wheel   steam   evil   squeeze   dream   these

List the words according to the 'ee' spellings.

Book 2

Timed reading of words with 'ee' spellings

real   me   keep   chief   leaf   Pete   steam   creep
shield   street   each   delete   steep   easy   belong
relax   seize   happy   field   reef   please   grief
free   messy   theme   treat   sneak   speech   thief
freedom   believe   wheat   cream   funny

1st try   Time:

---

real   me   keep   chief   leaf   Pete   steam   creep
shield   street   each   delete   steep   easy   belong
relax   seize   happy   field   reef   please   grief
free   messy   theme   treat   sneak   speech   thief
freedom   believe   wheat   cream   funny

2nd try   Time:

---

real   me   keep   chief   leaf   Pete   steam   creep
shield   street   each   delete   steep   easy   belong
relax   seize   happy   field   reef   please   grief
free   messy   theme   treat   sneak   speech   thief
freedom   believe   wheat   cream   funny

3rd try   Time:

This timed reading exercise is for the pupil to improve his/her reading speed and fluency. Ask the pupil to read the words as fast as he/she can. Record the time in the box. Repeat the exercise. This sheet can be cut or folded along the dotted lines to allow for different presentations.

Book 2

Chunking two-syllable words with 'ee'

freezing	free	zing	freezing
weaker			
compete			
belief			
creepy			
easy			
evil			
achieve			
shrieking			
agree			
beaten			
complete			
seizing			
delete			

Split the word into two syllables. Write each syllable in a box.
Write the whole word while saying the syllables.

Book 2

Phonic patterns

Colour in the words with 'ee' spellings.

extreme	beastly	wrench	wished
health	blend	sound	achieve
grieving	bread	sweeping	beaten
gone	stampede	release	dreaming
relax	hungry	evil	Wednesday

Fold this sheet on the dotted line. Read the words in the column on the left. Listen to the sounds in the words. Colour in the boxes with words that have 'ee' spellings. Repeat this in the other columns. Unfold the sheet and check that the correct words have been colored in.

Book 2

Is it true?

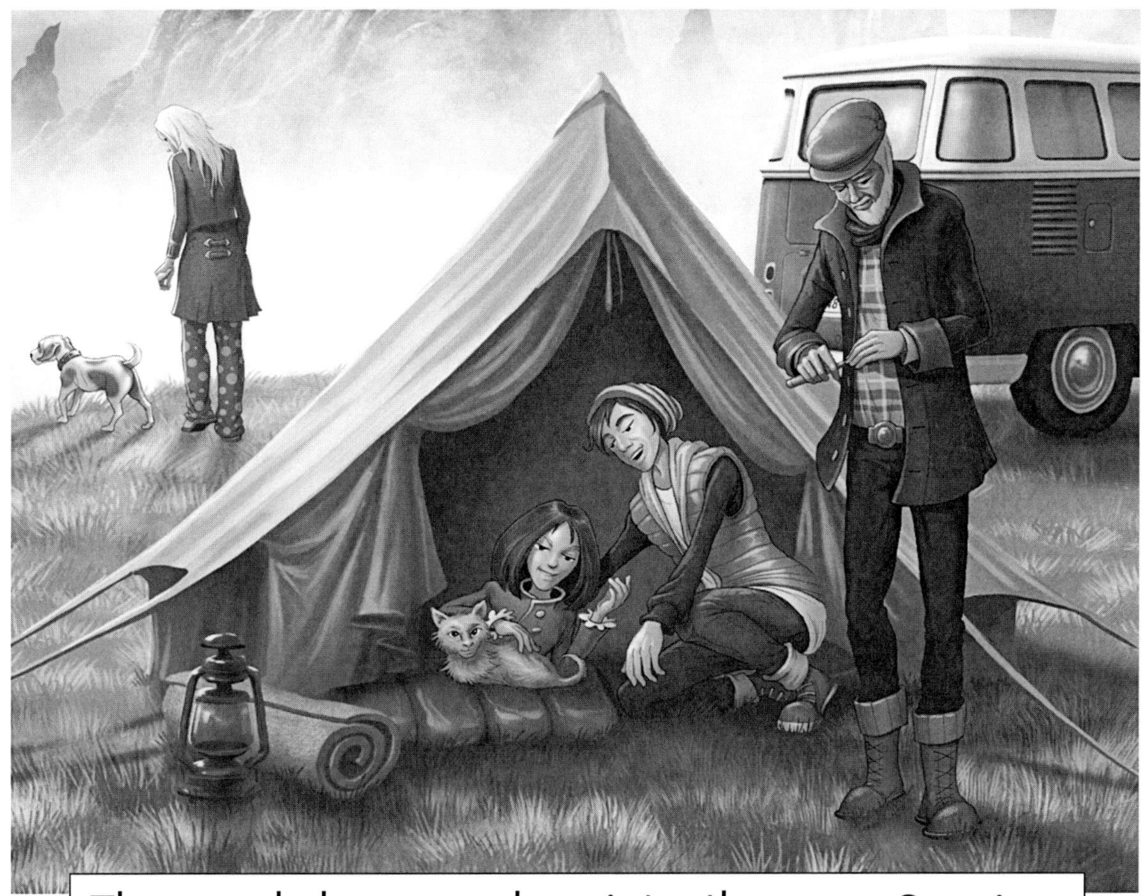

The workshop crashes into the sea. Gran's films have been lost. Then they spot a bag of the films in the sea! Grandpa and Snub take a raft out to look for them. They save a puppy from the sea. Snub plans to call him Otter. Grandpa sets up a tent for them to sleep in. Jack has a plan. He thinks Snub should go to Bayma Island with Gran!

There are **6** things in the story above that are not true. Can you spot them?

Ask the pupil to read the text carefully and circle any false information
that has been planted in the story.

Book 2

Picture the scene

Gran and Grandpa are standing at the edge of the sea.

Grandpa's van is parked behind him, on the left-hand side.

There are three huge rocky cliffs in the background.

There are four birds flying in the sky above them.

The sun is in the sky, on the left hand side of the picture.

Ask the pupil to read the text carefully and draw the details of the picture as described in the text.
Encourage them to read through all the text carefully before they begin working so they can plan
their drawing.
This sheet may be photocopied by the purchaser. © Phonic Books Ltd 2019

Book 2

Dictation

Skiffle swam back to the kayak, holding the kitten

__ __ __ __ __ __   __ __ __ __ ___ __ his __ ___ ___.

"__ __ must have __ ___ __   swept out to __ ___ by the

wild waves," said Grandpa.

Jack tucked him __ __ __ __ ___ __ his ___ ___ __.

"__ ___ __ __ __ __ __ __ __ ___," __ __ told him

__ __ __ __ __ __.

A __ __ ___ __ __ ___ __ of things

__ __ __ __ __ ___ __ __ __ filled the kayak. It __ ___ __ ___

as if the red box had sunk __ __ __ ___ ___ the waves.

Skiffle swam back to the kayak, holding the kitten **g e n t l y   b e t w ee n** his **t ee th**.

"**H e** must have **b ee n** swept out to **s ea** by the wild waves," said Grandpa.

Jack tucked him **b e t w ee n** his **kn ee s**.

"**K ee p   b r ea th i ng**," **h e** told him **s o f t l y**.

A **m e ss y h ea p** of things **c o m p l e t e l y** filled the kayak. It **s ee m ed** as if the red box

had sunk **b e n ea th** the waves.

Use the text at the bottom of the page for dictation. The section for dictation can either be cut off
by the teacher or folded along the dotted line to allow the pupil to self-check their spellings on
completion.
Dictate the passage to the pupil. Ask them to spell the missing words, writing a sound on each line.
Explain that a longer line indicates a spelling with more than one letter e.g. s ee d.

Book 2

Punctuation exercise

Capital letters and full stops

snub was named after a monkey gran had filmed snub-nosed monkeys have little button noses and huddle up in a bunch to stop them freezing snub had a little button nose and she loved to snuggle up too jack picked her up as they ran

There are **5** capital letters and **4** full stops missing.

Did you spot them all?

Ask the pupil to read through the text and add in capital letters and full stops where necessary. Encourage the pupil to read aloud as this will help him/her identify where the sentences stop.

Book 2

Developing vocabulary: **frantic**

The word 'frantic' is used here in Book 2:

'Frantic' means desperate or wild with excitement, fear or pain.

Circle the word or phrase that could be replaced with the word 'frantic' in the following text:

The old man held his head in his hands. He had lost his keys! He felt very upset. "I think I dropped them in the street," he said. "I must go back and get them."

Can you write two different sentences of your own using the word 'frantic'?

1.

____

____

2.

____

____

Book 2

Character profile

Use the word bank to help you describe Jack.

kind　　hot dogs　　adventure　　jogging

having fun　　sailing　　sleeping　　brother　　looking after

Name ____________

Age ____________

Loves ________________________________

Hates ________________________________

Hobbies ________________________________

Favourite food ________________________________

This is a writing frame to help structure creative writing. Ask the pupil to use words from the word bank to help them create a character profile for Jack. They will know some things from the story, but encourage them to be creative in their answers and to try to write in full sentences, using capital letters and full stops. This framework can also be used as a planning document for a piece of free writing.

Book 2: Stepping stones reading game: 'ee' words

A game for 1–4 players: Play with counters and dice.

Players should read aloud the words that they land on at the end of each turn and follow the black and white direction arrows if they land on them.

This sheet may be photocopied by the purchaser. © Phonic Books Ltd 2019

Book 2

Non fiction:

Snub-nosed monkeys – Fact card

Snub-nosed monkeys live in Asia. They get their name because they have a short stump-like nose on a round face. Their nostrils are flat on their face. Research suggests that this nose has developed as a means of protecting the monkey's nose from frostbite as they live in very cold places. Local people sometimes say the monkeys are easy to find in the rain because water gets into their noses and makes them sneeze! They often have quite multi-coloured long, thick fur which helps keep them warm.

Snub-nosed monkeys can grow to a length of 51 to 83 cm and their tails can grow to almost 100cm long. They live very high up, in mountain forests. The areas they live in are very remote and are difficult for humans to access. They spend most of their lives in the trees. They are very sociable and live in large groups of up to 600 members. Groups tend to be more males than females. They are very territorial and defend their territory by shouting, either alone or in large numbers.

These monkeys eat mainly tree needles, bamboo buds, fruit and leaves. They generally give birth to one baby monkey at a time. The baby monkey can take six to seven years to become fully mature.

<u>Snub-nosed monkeys</u>

1.____

2.____

3.____

4.____

5.____

6.____

This sheet provides the information needed to make a fact card. Ask the pupil to read the text carefully and circle the information they will need to make their card. They will need to select six key facts for their card. Explain that they need to look for information that will be relevant. They can then use this information to create the card in the box below.

Book 2

Dice game: words with 'ee' spellings

⚀	⚁	⚂	⚃	⚄	⚅
free	eat	she	each	chief	teapot
funny	sheep	reach	heel	leap	leave
week	begin	shriek	we	relief	relax
beans	badly	ceiling	field	sleepy	evil
peach	greed	sunny	feeling	weak	peel

This game is for two players. Each player needs a batch of counters of one colour. The players take turns to throw the die. They read a word in the column that corresponds to the number on the die and place their counter on that word. The first to have three of his/her counters in a row in any direction is the winner.

Book 2

Spelling assessment for words with 'ee' spellings

1.

ee	ea	e	e–e	y	ie	ei
feet	sea	me	Pete	funny	chief	seize
sheep	meat	she	theme	happy	thief	ceiling
breed	bleak	relax	delete	floppy	shield	

2.

ee	ea	e	e–e	y	ie
greed	dream	evil	compete	badly	priest
agree	bleach	begin	complete	angry	piece
screech	scream	belong	athlete	hungry	shriek

These lists can be used as a spelling assessment at the end of each book. The teacher can add words from list 2 for pupils who are ready for that stage. When dictating a word, first say the word on its own. Next, say a sentence with the word in it (to put the word in the context of a sentence) and then repeat the word. This ensures that the pupil has heard the word correctly e.g. "Funny. The joke was very funny. Funny."

Island Adventure Series
Book 3: Coast to Coast

Contents

Book 3
Blending and segmenting: 'oe'

bow	b	ow		
no				
hope		o		e
toe				
most				
roast				
slope				
foe				
stone				
groans				
snowing				
homeless				
joking				

Blend the sounds into a word. Segment the word into sounds by writing one sound in each square.
Split vowel spellings (o-e) are represented by half squares linked together.

Book 3
Reading and sorting words with 'oe' spellings

o	oa	ow	o-e	oe

rope	go	hole	bow
toe	bold	bone	coat
joke	most	load	home
groan	hold	float	goes
snow	spoke	shoal	broken
know	soap	Rome	hero
roast	flow	goat	note
alone	toast	crow	Book 3 Reading cards 'oe' spellings

Photocopy this page onto card and cut into reading cards.
Store cards in an envelope and stick the label on the front for reference.
Can also be photocopied twice on different coloured card and cut into cards to make a simple matching game.

Reading and spelling words with 'oe' spellings

ow	oa	o–e

o	oe

blow   groan   so   snow   woe   roast   hope   road
show   joke   no   throat   foe   grow   bone   bloat
go   drove   toe   throw   spoke

List the words according to the 'oe' spellings.

Book 3

Timed reading of words with 'oe' spellings

hope   road   blow   so   snow   woe   roast
groan   show   no   throw   foe   grow   bone
bloat   go   rove   toe   flow   spoke   pole   coat
mole   crow   moan   slope   goat   toad   groan
low   know   roll   hole   cope   most

1st try   Time:

- -

hope   road   blow   so   snow   woe   roast
groan   show   no   throw   foe   grow   bone
bloat   go   rove   toe   flow   spoke   pole   coat
mole   crow   moan   slope   goat   toad   groan
low   know   roll   hole   cope   most

2nd try   Time:

- -

hope   road   blow   so   snow   woe   roast
groan   show   no   throw   foe   grow   bone
bloat   go   rove   toe   flow   spoke   pole   coat
mole   crow   moan   slope   goat   toad   groan
low   know   roll   hole   cope   most

3rd try   Time:

This timed reading exercise is for the pupil to improve his/her reading speed and fluency. Ask the pupil to read the words as fast as he/she can. Record the time in the box. Repeat the exercise. This sheet can be cut or folded along the dotted lines to allow for different presentations.

Book 3

Chunking two-syllable words with 'oe'

widow	wid	ow	widow
open			
hopeless			
moaning			
narrow			
woeful			
joking			
lonely			
boastful			
tiptoe			
borrow			
hero			
homeless			
oboe			

Split the word into two syllables. Write each syllable in a box.
Write the whole word while saying the syllables.

Book 3

Phonic patterns

Colour in the words with 'oe' spellings.

cotton	below	throat	spotted
shopping	crow	belong	float
joking	got	cope	snowman
pillow	angry	follow	spoke
rope	boast	broken	job

Fold this sheet on the dotted line. Read the words in the column on the left. Listen to the sounds in the words. Colour in the lozenges with words that have 'oe' spellings. Repeat this in the other columns. Unfold the sheet and check that the correct words have been coloured in.

Is it true?

Jack and Gran set off for the mainland in a speedboat. The sea is rough and choppy. A climber calls to them from a sea stack. He has dropped his hat and can't reach it. Jack jumps from the boat to help him. The man is very grateful and is able to finish his climb. They reach the mainland. Gran collects up an old camper van. A massive rock rolls down the hill and crashes into them. Jack is excited to see it has carvings on it. He thinks it looks like a football!

There are **5** things in the story above that are not true. Can you spot them?

Ask the pupil to read the text carefully and circle any false information
that has been planted in the story.

Book 3

Picture the scene

Gran and Snub are on top of a long brick wall at the harbour.

Grandpa's rowing boat is in the sea in front of the wall.

Skiffle the dog is behind Snub.

The moon is high in the sky, behind Gran.

Snub is handing Gran a shell necklace.

Book 3

Dictation

The man reached the top of the stack. He swung his way back down on a __ __ __ __ until he got to his __ ___ __. Gran __ __ ___ __ ___. "Please stick to running and __ __ __' __ take up that hobby," she __ __ __ __. The wind was still __ __ ___ __ ___ when they reached the mainland. "I keep an __ __ __ truck in that shed," said Gran. "We'll stay in the __ __ __ __ __ at the top of the cliff until the plane leaves __ __ __ __ ___ ___. The __ ___ __ up the cliff __ __ __ __ ___ steeply. The truck __ __ ___ __ ___ as it went __ __ ___ __ __ up the hill.

The man reached the top of the stack. He swung his way back down on a **r o p e** until he got to his **b oa t**.

Gran **g r oa n ed**. "Please stick to running and **d o n't** take up that hobby, she **j o k ed**.

The wind was still **b l ow i ng** when they reached the mainland.

"I keep an **o l d** truck in that shed," said Gran. "We'll stay in the **h o t e l** at the top of the cliff until the

plane leaves **t o m o rr ow**.

The **r oa d** up the cliff **s l o p ed** steeply. The truck **g r oa n ed** as it went **s l ow l y** up the hill.

Use the text at the bottom of the page for dictation. The section for dictation can either be cut off by the teacher or folded along the dotted line to allow the pupil to self-check their spellings on completion.
Dictate the passage to the pupil. Ask them to spell the missing words, writing a sound on each line.
Explain that a longer line indicates a spelling with more than one letter e.g. b l ow.

Book 3

Punctuation exercise

Capital letters, commas and full stops

snub gave jack and gran lucky necklaces she had made with shells skiffle stayed close to her "he's not keen on getting back into the sea" explained snub as she stroked him "it's a bit too wet and there are no dog bones in it"

There are **7** capital letters, **1** comma and **4** full stops missing.

Did you spot them all?

Ask the pupil to read through the text and add in capital letters and full stops where necessary. Encourage the pupil to read aloud as this will help him/her identify where the sentences stop.

Book 3

Developing vocabulary: **nipped**

The word 'nipped' is used here in Book 3:

'Nipped' is another word for
taking small bites of something.

Circle the word or phrase that could be replaced with the word 'nipped' in the following text:

The puppy was still young and very playful. He nibbled Yusuf's fingers when they played.

Can you write two different sentences of your own using the word 'nipped'?

1.

____

____

2.

____

____

Book 3

Character profile

Use the word bank to help you describe Grandpa.

mending things honey cake boats caring

skipping old red van runner brave

Name _____________

Age _____________

Loves _________________________________

Hates _________________________________

Hobbies _______________________________

Favourite food _________________________

This is a writing frame to help structure creative writing. Ask the pupil to use words from the word bank to help them create a character profile for Grandpa. They will know some things from the story, but encourage them to be creative in their answers and to try to write in full sentences, using capital letters and full stops. This framework can also be used as a planning document for a piece of free writing.

Book 3: Stepping stones reading game: 'oe' words

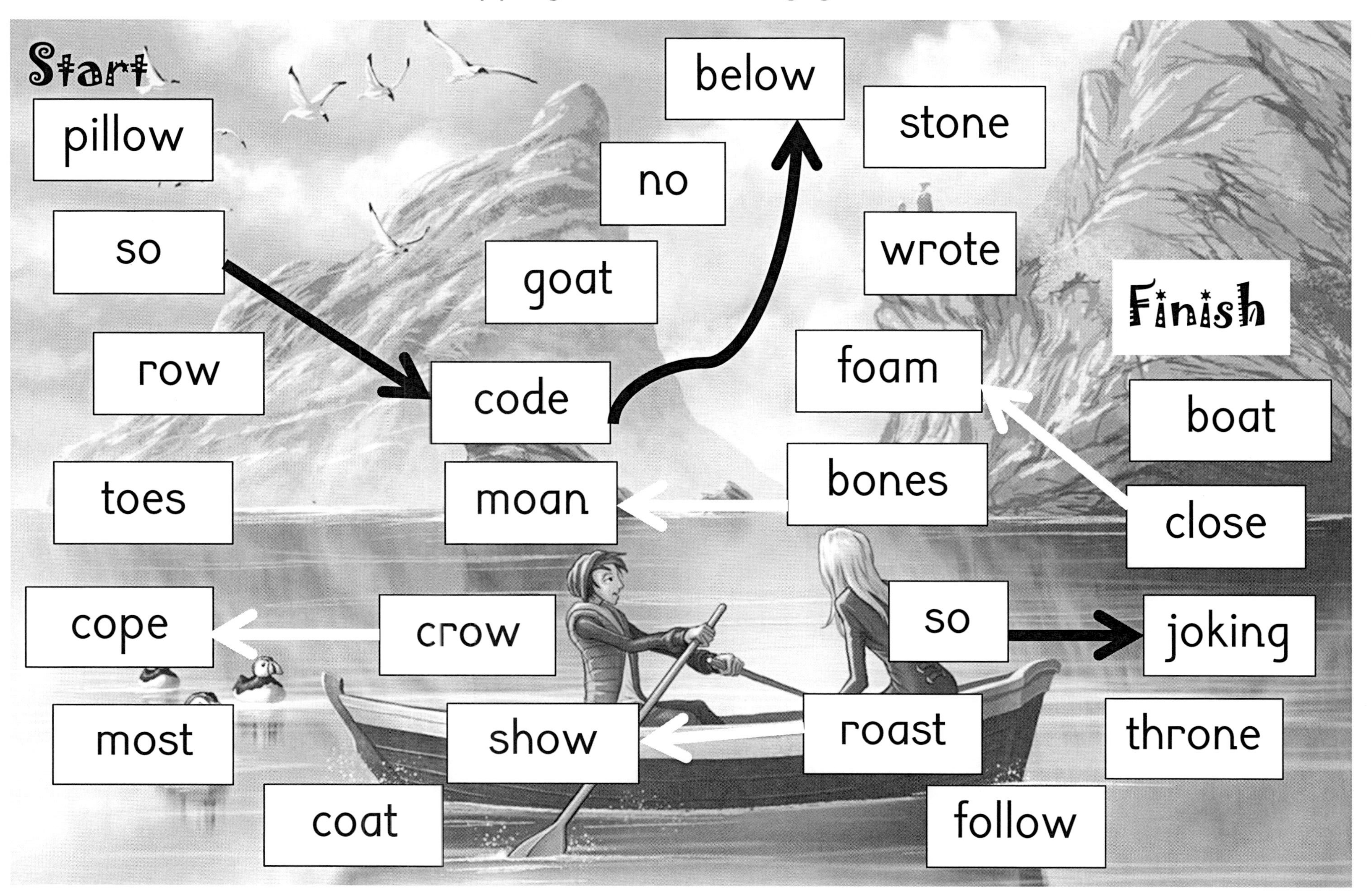

A game for 1–4 players: Play with counters and dice.

Players should read aloud the words that they land on at the end of each turn and follow the black and white direction arrows if they land on them.

This sheet may be photocopied by the purchaser. © Phonic Books Ltd 2019

Book 3

Non fiction:

Sea stacks – Factual postcard

A sea stack is a very steep, vertical column of rock in the sea. It is formed by erosion from the waves that causes a piece of the headland to break away from the mainland. It will always remain near the coast.

Sea stacks are formed when the force of the water crashing against the rocks of the mainland causes cracks to appear in the cliffs. The water then gradually weakens these cracks until sometimes a part of the headland breaks away. Sea stacks are very popular with climbers for rock climbing. They can also provide important nesting places for birds. Sometimes erosion leads to the stack being connected to the headland by an archway of rock, before this eventually wears away and the sea stack becomes a separate rock formation.

The tallest sea stack in the world is called Ball's Pyramid. It is in the Pacific Ocean and measures a staggering 562 metres high! It was formed over 6 million years ago. It is surrounded by very rough seas which makes approaching it very difficult.

Hi Mum,

You'll never guess what Gran and I saw today!

Love from Jack x

This sheet provides the information needed to create a factual postcard. Ask the pupil to read the text carefully and circle the information they will need to make their postcard. Explain that they need to look for information that will be useful for someone who knows nothing about sea stacks. They can then use this information to create the postcard in the box below.

Book 3

Dice game: words with 'oe' spellings

(1)	(2)	(3)	(4)	(5)	(6)
toad	coast	poach	low	show	flown
hope	choke	spoke	go	hero	no
smoke	joke	blow	groan	slowly	bones
throne	so	road	snow	elbow	arrow
tiptoe	boats	soap	woe	home	pillow

This game is for two players. Each player needs a batch of counters of one colour. The players take turns to throw the die. They read a word in the column that corresponds to the number on the die and place their counter on that word. The first to have three of his/her counters in a row in any direction is the winner.

Book 3

Spelling assessment for words with 'oe' spellings

1.

oa	**ow**	**o–e**	**o**	**oe**
road	low	home	go	toe
boast	show	choke	so	woe
poach	blown	smoke	hero	foe

2.

oa	**ow**	**o–e**	**o**	**oe**
groans	window	lonely	going	tiptoe
floating	shadow	hopeful	joking	woeful
boasted	slowly	stroke	broken	

These lists can be used as a spelling assessment at the end of each book. The teacher can add words from list 2 for pupils who are ready for that stage. When dictating a word, first say the word on its own. Next, say a sentence with the word in it (to put the word in the context of a sentence) and then repeat the word. This ensures that the pupil has heard the word correctly, e.g. "Road. The boy ran down the road. Road."

Island Adventure Series
Book 4: A World Away

Contents

Book 4
Blending and segmenting: 'er'

sir	s	ir	
fur			
term			
word			
earn			
church			
twirl			
nerve			
worth			
learns			
burst			
skirt			
world			

Blend the sounds into a word. Segment the word into sounds by writing one sound in each square.

Book 4
Reading and sorting words with 'er' spellings

er	ur	ir	or	ear

her	first	burp	worm
world	earn	purse	jerk
early	bird	serve	turn
worth	heard	curl	kerb
dirty	work	verse	learn
curse	worth	birth	whirl
murder	sister	stir	expert
search	worship	disturb	Book 4 Reading cards 'er' spellings

Photocopy this page onto card and cut into reading cards.
Store cards in an envelope and stick the label on the front for reference.
Can also be photocopied twice on different coloured card and cut into cards to make a simple matching game.

Reading and spelling words with 'er' spellings

er	ur	ir
______	______	______
______	______	______
______	______	______
______	______	______
______	______	______

or	ear
______	______
______	______
______	______

her   first   burp   worm   world   earn   purse   bird
serve   turn   birth   heard   dirty   work   sister
verb   earth   burnt   fur   girl   verse

List the words according to the 'er' spellings.

Book 4

Timed reading of words with 'er' spellings

her   fir   earn   word   hurt   shirt   turn   fern
yearn   work   learn   world   burp   sister
further   early   dirty   worth   girl   church
search   enter   worm   term   skirt   germ   heard
father   over   firm   burnt   verse   worse

1st try   **Time:**

---

her   fir   earn   word   hurt   shirt   turn   fern
yearn   work   learn   world   burp   sister
further   early   dirty   worth   girl   church
search   enter   worm   term   skirt   germ   heard
father   over   firm   burnt   verse   worse

2nd try   **Time:**

---

her   fir   earn   word   hurt   shirt   turn   fern
yearn   work   learn   world   burp   sister
further   early   dirty   worth   girl   church
search   enter   worm   term   skirt   germ   heard
father   over   firm   burnt   verse   worse

3rd try   **Time:**

This timed reading exercise is for the pupil to improve his/her reading speed and fluency. Ask the pupil to read the words as fast as he/she can. Record the time in the box. Repeat the exercise. This sheet can be cut or folded along the dotted lines to allow for different presentations.

Book 4

Chunking two-syllable words with 'er'

disturb	dis	turb	disturb
worship			
person			
thirteen			
murder			
earning			
thirsty			
expert			
early			
worker			
birthday			
further			
worthless			
permit			

Split the word into two syllables. Write each syllable in a box.
Write the whole word while saying the syllables.

Book 4

Phonic patterns

Colour in the words with 'er' spellings.

further	early	bunting	circle
blend	worth	butter	plastic
jelly	purple	church	birthday
heard	word	first	nurse
instead	bubble	blister	murmur

Fold this sheet on the dotted line. Read the words in the column on the left. Listen to the sounds in the words. Colour in the lozenges with words that have 'er' spellings. Repeat this in the other columns. Unfold the sheet and check the correct words have been coloured in.

Is it true?

Gran is happy to let Ash join them on the trip. They catch a ferry to the island. It is boiling hot when they arrive. Jack and Ash go for a swim. They discover a huge pile of plastic bags. Jack makes a model of a turtle to show Snub. He decorates it with his wrist watch. An old lady appears and gathers up all the plastic bottles.

There are **5** things in the story above that are not true. Can you spot them?

Ask the pupil to read the text carefully and circle any false information
that has been planted in the story.

Book 4

Picture the scene

There is a plane behind Gran, Ash and Jack.

The entrance to the airport is on the left-hand side of the picture.

Gran and Jack are pulling small suitcases.

Ash is carrying a bag.

It is raining.

Ask the student to read the text carefully and draw the details of the picture as described in the text. Encourage them to read through all the text carefully before they begin working so they can plan their drawing.

Book 4

Dictation

The beach was amazing. Waves lapped against the
__ __ __ __ ___ sand. Ash was a __ __ ___ ___ like Jack.

They ran __ ___ ___ ___ and __ ___ ___ ___ along the

beach.

"This bit is __ __ __ ___ __ __ __," yelled Ash. Then Jack spotted

an odd heap of things, __ __ __ ___ ___ __ ___ in the sun.

As they got __ __ __ __ ___ they saw it was a

__ __ __ __ __ ___ of plastic bottles, sitting neatly in the sand.

"Snub makes great things with junk like this that keeps floating in

from the sea," said Jack. "Let's make __ ___ a __ ___ __ ___."

The beach was amazing. Waves lapped against the **s i l v er** sand. Ash was a **r u nn er** like Jack.

They ran **f ur th er** and **f ur th er** along the beach.

"This bit is **d e s er t e d**," yelled Ash. Then Jack spotted an odd heap of things, **g l i tt er i ng** in the sun.

As they got **c l o s er** they saw it was a **c l u s t er** of plastic bottles, sitting neatly in the sand.

"Snub makes great things with junk like this that keeps floating in from the sea," said Jack. "Let's make **h er** a **t ur t le**."

Use the text at the bottom of the page for dictation. The section for dictation can either be cut off by the teacher or folded along the dotted line to allow the pupil to self-check their spellings on completion.
Dictate the passage to the pupil. Ask them to spell the missing words, writing a sound on each line.
Explain that a longer line indicates a spelling with more than one letter e.g. <u>w</u> or <u>d</u>.

Book 4

Punctuation exercise

Capital letters and speech marks

ash's dad ran up. mack! said gran as she hugged him. she and mack were old friends. mack groaned when he saw the truck. i am so sorry! at least let me make you supper. we have a camper van and i make a great burger.

There are **10** capital letters and

2 sets of speech marks missing.

Did you spot them all?

Ask the pupil to read through the text and add in capital letters and speech marks where necessary. Encourage the pupil to read aloud as this will help him/her identify where the punctuation occurs.

Book 4

Developing vocabulary: **cluster**

The word 'cluster' is used here in Book 4:

Circle the word or phrase that could be replaced with the word 'cluster' in the following text:

The boy rubbed his eyes. He looked around him. A group of children were sitting and chatting on the beach.

Can you write two different sentences of your own using the word 'cluster'?

1.

____

____

2.

____

____

Book 4

Character profile

Use the word bank to help you describe Gran.

taking pictures
prawn salad
dancing
animal lover
having fun
Spain
grandmother
artist
camping

Name ___________

Age ___________

Loves ____

Hates ____

Hobbies ______________________________________

Favourite food _________________________________

This is a writing frame to help structure creative writing. Ask the pupil to use words from the word bank to help them create a character profile for Gran. They will know some things from the story, but encourage them to be creative in their answers and to try to write in full sentences, using capital letters and full stops. This framework can also be used as a planning document for a piece of free writing.

Book 4: Stepping stones reading game: 'er' words

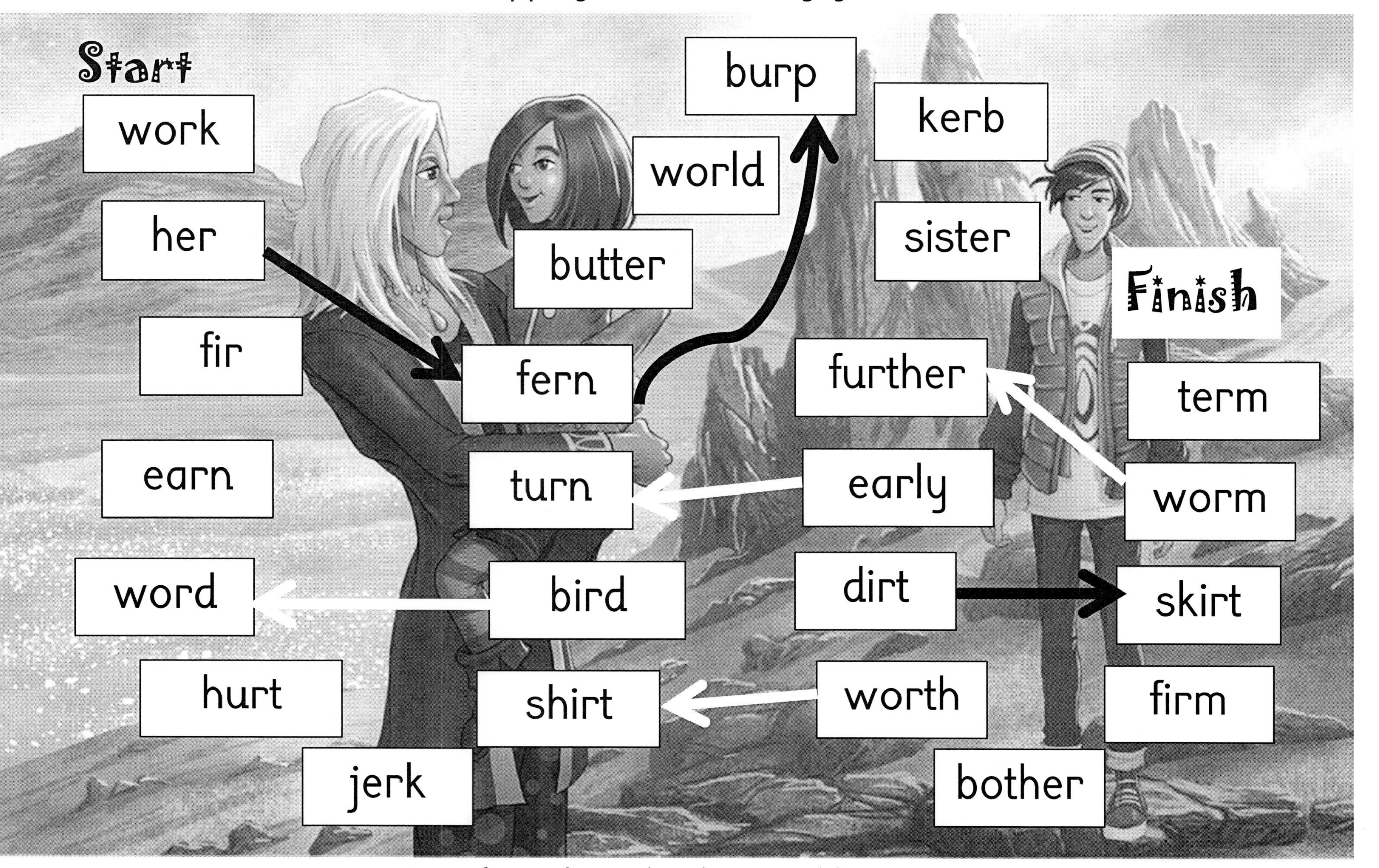

A game for 1–4 players: Play with counters and dice.

Players should read aloud the words that they land on at the end of each turn and follow the black and white direction arrows if they land on them.

Book 4

Non fiction:

Marine plastic pollution – Poster

The earth's oceans are struggling to cope with the amount of plastic that ends up in the sea every year. On average 8 million tonnes of plastic currently ends up in the sea. Research has suggested that if this continues we run the risk of ending up with more plastic than fish in the sea by 2050.

Plastic is a massive problem in the sea. Marine birds and animals can end up entangled in it or poisoned by it. Some plastic is visible as it floats on the top of the ocean. Under the surface there is tonnes more broken down plastic.

How can we help? Raising awareness of the problem is a key concern for environmentalists. Decreasing our use of plastic and improving the way waste plastic is managed all helps make a huge difference. Plastic is a remarkable material with many benefits, but a large amount of it ends up in landfill – often after just one use. 80% of the plastic in the oceans started out as landfill.

Coastal clear-up involving members of the community can help clear some waste plastic from the oceans and beaches.

Plastic straws are a large problem as they are only used once and then thrown away. Many companies and businesses are now turning away from plastic straws and adopting paper straws or drinks with no straws at all.

Marine Plastic pollution

Use the information above to create an eye-catching poster raising awareness of marine pollution.

Posters have to catch the eye very quickly. People may often see them very quickly in passing (for example on a station escalator) and they need to grasp the main message from them very quickly.

Remember a small amount of information presented in an eye-catching way that captures people's attention is likely to have the biggest impact.

Choose one to three key facts from the information above to give your poster impact.

Use any illustrations to help convey your message.

This sheet provides the information needed to make a poster. Ask the pupil to read the text carefully and circle the information they will need to make their poster. Explain that they need to look for information that will capture the most attention. They can then use this information to create the poster on a piece of paper.

Book 4

Dice game: words with 'er' spellings

(1)	(2)	(3)	(4)	(5)	(6)
girl	burnt	verse	worse	her	fir
earn	word	hurt	shirt	burns	work
turn	fur	early	dirty	worth	firm
bitter	search	enter	purple	matter	germ
worm	skirt	over	father	anger	potter

This game is for two players. Each player needs a batch of counters of one colour. The players take turns to throw the die. They read a word or letter in the column that corresponds to the number on the die and place their counter on that word. The first to have three of his/her counters in a row in any direction is the winner.

Book 4

Spelling assessment for words with 'er' spellings

1.

er	**ir**	**ur**	**ear**	**or**
her	sir	hurt	pearl	word
serve	bird	curl	search	work
nerves	first	turns	heard	worms

2.

er	**ir**	**ur**	**ear**	**or**
over	stir	burnt	early	world
finger	twirl	church	earned	worth
hunger	birthday	disturb	earnest	worse

These lists can be used as a spelling assessment at the end of each book. The teacher can add words from list 2 for pupils who are ready for that stage. When dictating a word, first say the word on its own. Next, say a sentence with the word in it (to put the word in the context of a sentence) and then repeat the word. This ensures that the pupil has heard the word correctly, e.g. "Hurt. The girl hurt her leg when she fell. Hurt."

Island Adventure Series
Book 5: Sounds and Shadows
Contents

Book 5
Blending and segmenting: 'ow'

out	ou	t			
how					
loud					
town					
pouch					
brown					
sound					
drown					
mouth					
scowl					
ground					
howling					
about					

Blend the sounds into a word. Segment the word into sounds by writing one sound in each square.

Book 5
Blending and segmenting: 'oi'

toy	t	oy			
oil					
boy					
coin					
soya					
voice					
enjoy					
spoil					
loyal					
avoid					
annoy					
toilet					
employ					

Blend the sounds into a word. Segment the word into sounds by writing one sound in each square.

Book 5: Reading and sorting words with 'ow' and 'oi' spellings

ow		**ou**	
howl	round	aloud	tower
ouch	power	shout	frown
allow	spout	shower	bound

oi		**oy**	
boy	enjoy	point	toilet
soil	toy	royal	voice
annoy	coin	destroy	spoilt

Photocopy this page onto card and cut out the words. Read and sort the cards out according to the 'ow' and 'oi' headings.

Book 5
Reading and spelling words with 'ow' and 'oi' spellings

ow

____

____

____

____

____

ou

____

____

____

____

____

shout   how   power   mound   sound   scout   clown
brown   drown   house

oi

____

____

____

____

oy

____

____

____

____

toy   spoil   enjoy   point   ploy   foil
avoid   boy

List the words according to the 'ow' and 'oi' spellings.

Book 5

Timed reading of words with 'ow' spellings

fowl   loud   round   town   pout   house   mount
allow   proud   howl   crowd   how   sound   noun
vowel   spout   frown   brow   towel   growl
found   hound   brown   wow   cloud   clown
ground   mouse   scout   discount   trowel

1st try   **Time:**

---

fowl   loud   round   town   pout   house   mount
allow   proud   howl   crowd   how   sound   noun
vowel   spout   frown   brow   towel   growl
found   hound   brown   wow   cloud   clown
ground   mouse   scout   discount   trowel

2nd try   **Time:**

---

fowl   loud   round   town   pout   house   mount
allow   proud   howl   crowd   how   sound   noun
vowel   spout   frown   brow   towel   growl
found   hound   brown   wow   cloud   clown
ground   mouse   scout   discount   trowel

3rd try   **Time:**

This timed reading exercise is for the pupil to improve his/her reading speed and fluency. Ask the pupil to read the words as fast as he/she can. Record the time in the box. Repeat the exercise. This sheet can be cut or folded along the dotted lines to allow for different presentations.

Book 5

Timed reading of words with 'oi' spellings

toil boy noise toy spoil soya boil
voice joy coin poise annoy coil point
oil joint toilet royal oyster employ
enjoy foil loyal poison avoid ointment
decoy destroy soil boiling

1st try   Time:

----

toil boy noise toy spoil soya boil
voice joy coin poise annoy coil point
oil joint toilet royal oyster employ
enjoy foil loyal poison avoid ointment
decoy destroy soil boiling

2nd try   Time:

----

toil boy noise toy spoil soya boil
voice joy coin poise annoy coil point
oil joint toilet royal oyster employ
enjoy foil loyal poison avoid ointment
decoy destroy soil boiling

3rd try   Time:

Book 5

Chunking two-syllable words with 'ow'

loudest	loud	est	loudest
power			
pouting			
drowsy			
voucher			
outing			
grounded			
towel			
bouncy			
howling			
mouthful			
flower			
rebound			
crowded			

Split the word into two syllables. Write each syllable in a box.
Write the whole word while saying the syllables.

Book 5

Chunking two-syllable words with 'oi'

employ	*em*	*ploy*	*employ*
oily			
convoy			
poison			
toilet			
destroy			
avoid			
decoy			
noisy			
annoy			
boiling			
royal			
ointment			
enjoy			

Split the word into two syllables. Write each syllable in a box.
Write the whole word while saying the syllables.

Book 5
Reading and sorting words with <ow> spelling

sn**ow**	c**ow**

howl	growl	mow	bow
now	blow	low	tow
flow	know	crown	crow
allow	glow	brow	town
slow	show	brown	fowl
jowl	power	bowl	shown
vow	throw	trowel	towel
down	shower	yellow	flower

Photocopy this page onto card and cut out the words. Read and sort the cards out according to the sounds of the <ow> spelling. The two sounds are 'snow' and 'cow'.

Book 5

Phonic patterns

Colour in <u>only</u> words with the spelling <ow> that is pronounced 'ow' as in 'clown'.

blow	down	throw	crown
frown	crowd	crow	howl
show	mellow	shower	tower
drown	flower	owl	know
how	town	flow	low

Fold this sheet on the dotted line. Read the words in the column on the left. Listen to the sounds in the words. Colour in the lozenges with words that have the spelling <ow> that is pronounced 'ow' as in 'clown'. Repeat this in the other columns. Unfold the sheet and check the correct words have been coloured in.

This sheet may be photocopied by the purchaser. © Phonic Books Ltd 2019

Is it true?

Danny shows Jack and Ash how to make plastic boats with the old plastic bottles. They sleep in a house made of plastic bottles! Next morning they set off for the beach. Jack stops to take a photo of a parrot. They get lost. Jack climbs a tree to try and reach some wild honey. At the end of the day they find a cave to sleep in.

There are **4** things in the story above that are not true. Can you spot them?

Ask the pupil to read the text carefully and circle any false information
that has been planted in the story.

Book 5

Picture the scene

There is a big campfire at the front of the picture.

There is a flat pan of food cooking on the fire.

There is a fence behind the characters.

The trunks of trees can be seen behind the fence.

The moon is visible between the trees.

Ask the pupil to read the text carefully and draw the details of the picture as described in the text.
Encourage them to read through all the text carefully before they begin working so they can plan
their drawing.

Book 5

Dictation

They all set off into the forest. There was so much to see. Ash posed with a __ __ ____ ____. Jack gave a mock __ ____. "The __ ____ __ __ queen of the forest," he joked, "and I am your __ ____ __ __ servant."

When they got going again they saw the track had split into three. Jack __ __ ____ __ ____. They'd been left behind. Where were Danny and Gran?

"Danny!" he ____ ____ __ ____ __ ____ __ __ __.

Ash __ ____ __ __ ____ to the left. "I think they went this way. If we run we'll catch them up."

They all set off into the forest. There was so much to see. Ash posed with a **f l ow er**. Jack gave a mock **b ow**.

"The **r oy a l** queen of the forest," he joked, "and I am your **l oy a l** servant."

When they got going again they saw the track had split into three. Jack **f r ow n ed**. They'd been left behind. Where were Danny and Gran?

"Danny!" he **sh ou t ed   l ou d l y**.

Ash **p oi n t ed** to the left. "I think they went this way. If we run we'll catch them up."

Use the text at the bottom of the page for dictation. The section for dictation can either be cut off by the teacher or folded along the dotted line to allow the pupil to self-check their spellings on completion.

Dictate the passage to the pupil. Ask them to spell the missing words, writing a sound on each line. Explain that a longer line indicates a spelling with more than one letter e.g. h ow l.

Book 5

Punctuation exercise

Question marks

jack stretched. jet lag had suddenly hit him. gran patted his hand.

"sleep now, jack" she said. "we're all going into the forest tomorrow." jack gazed around him with a puzzled frown. were they going to sleep on the ground

There are 8 capital letters and 1 question mark missing.

Did you spot them all?

Ask the pupil to read through the text and add in capital letters and a question mark where necessary. Encourage the pupil to read aloud as this will help him/her identify where the punctuation occurs

Book 5

Developing vocabulary: **tucked**

The word 'tucked' is used here in Book 5:

Circle the word or phrase that could be replaced with the word 'tucked' in the following text:

He was so proud of his birthday card. He tiptoed up to the doorway and placed it carefully into the letterbox.

Can you write two different sentences of your own using the word 'tucked'?

1.

____

____

2.

____

____

Book 5

Character profile

Use the word bank to help you describe Ash.

making clothes   artist   travelling   animal lover
running   salad   environment   beach

Name _____________

Age _____________

Loves _______________________________________

Hates _______________________________________

Hobbies _____________________________________

Favourite food ______________________________

This is a writing frame to help structure creative writing. Ask the pupil to use words from the word bank to help them create a character profile for Ash. They will know some things from the story, but encourage them to be creative in their answers and to try to write in full sentences, using capital letters and full stops. This framework can also be used as a planning document for a piece of free writing.

Book 5: Stepping stones reading game: 'ow' and 'oi' words

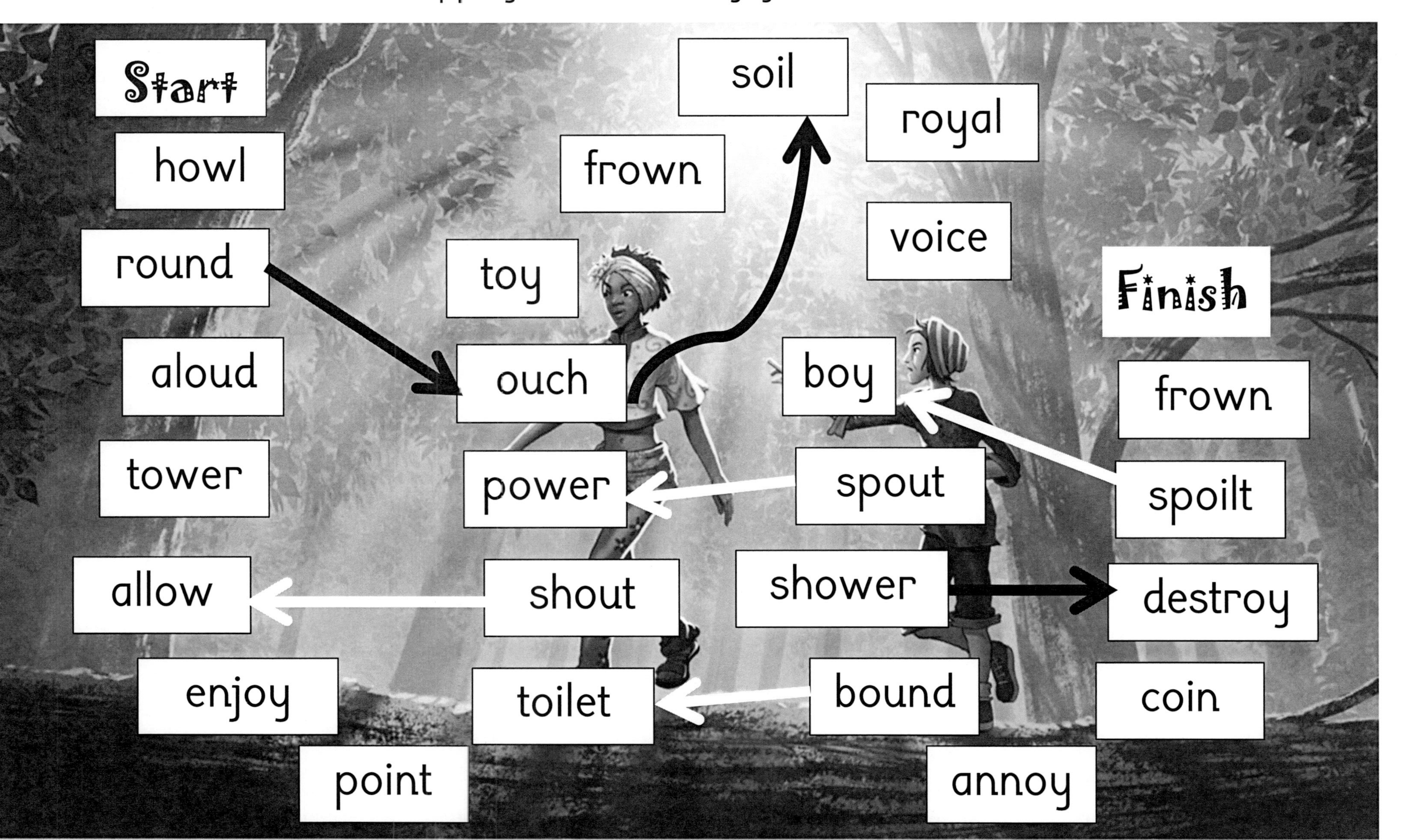

A game for 1–4 players: Play with counters and dice.

Players should read aloud the words that they land on at the end of each turn and follow the black and white direction arrows if they land on them.

This sheet may be photocopied by the purchaser. © Phonic Books Ltd 2019

Book 5

Non fiction:

Plastic bottle greenhouses – Letter to parents

It is possible to make a great greenhouse using plastic bottles. The bottles are threaded onto bamboo poles and then secured to metal or wooden posts. It can take up to 1,000 bottles to create a greenhouse! Making one as a group is a great way of using plastic bottles that would otherwise end up as landfill.

Here are the steps to make a plastic bottle greenhouse

1. Remove the lids and labels from the bottles.

2. Cut the bottom of each bottle with scissors. Keep the top end of the bottle on as this helps keep the bottles in position on the pole.

3. Fix four metal or wooden posts into the ground to make the corners of the greenhouse.

4. Use bamboo canes to string the bottles onto as the sides of the greenhouse. Make sure they are long enough to reach the corner posts.

5. Thread the bottles through the bamboo canes to make long lines of bottles. The bottles will all slot up against each other on the canes.

6. When the canes are all threaded with bottles they can be nailed or secured to the four corner poles to make the walls of the greenhouse.

7. A simple roof can be made with wood or more threaded bamboo canes of bottles.

Dear parents,

This sheet provides the information needed to write a letter to parents at school asking them to send in plastic bottles. Ask the pupil to read the text carefully and circle the information they will need in their letter. Explain that they need to look for information that will explain what the bottles are going to be used for and how the greenhouse will be made.

Book 5

Dice game: words with 'ow' and 'oi' spellings

⚀ (1)	⚁ (2)	⚂ (3)	⚃ (4)	⚄ (5)	⚅ (6)
hound	choice	toy	boil	voice	round
about	clown	trout	foil	ploy	brow
point	how	found	brown	boiled	loud
allow	soil	town	mouth	coin	power
spoil	now	enjoy	oil	owl	our

This game is for two players. Each player needs a batch of counters of one colour. The players take turns to throw the die. They read a word or letter in the column that corresponds to the number on the die and place their counter on that word. The first to have three of his/her counters in a row in any direction is the winner.

Book 5

Spelling assessment for words with 'ow' and 'oi' spellings

1.

ow	**ou**	**oi**	**oy**
how	out	coin	toy
brow	bout	boils	boys
crown	spout	spoil	cloy

2.

ow	**ou**	**oi**	**oy**
powder	ground	pointed	employ
frowning	rounders	boiling	destroy
cowshed	astounded	rejoice	enjoyed

These lists can be used as a spelling assessment at the end of each book. The teacher can add words from list 2 for pupils who are ready for that stage. When dictating a word, first say the word on its own. Next, say a sentence with the word in it (to put the word in the context of a sentence) and then repeat the word. This ensures that the pupil has heard the word correctly, e.g. "Crown. The queen placed the crown on her head. Crown."

Island Adventure Series
Book 6: A Shrewd Route

Contents

Book 6
Blending and segmenting: 'oo'

too	t	oo					
youth	☐	☐	☐				
rude	☐	u	☐	e			
chew	☐	☐					
group	☐	☐	☐	☐			
scoop	☐	☐	☐	☐			
brute	☐	☐	☐	☐	☐		
threw	☐	☐	☐				
include	☐	☐	☐	☐	☐	☐	☐
truth	☐	☐	☐	☐			
blue	☐	☐	☐				
clueless	☐	☐	☐	☐	☐	☐	
July	☐	☐	☐	☐			

Blend the sounds into a word. Segment the word into sounds by writing one sound in each square.
Split vowel spellings (u–e) are represented by half squares linked together.

Book 6
Reading and sorting words with 'oo' spellings

oo	ue	u-e	ew	ou	u

drew	proof	loose	crew
shampoo	scuba	coupon	plume
pool	rude	blue	group
grew	shoot	super	youth
flew	rule	true	brutal
glue	scoop	crude	chew
route	judo	smooth	sue
brute	jewel	include	Book 6 Reading cards 'oo' spellings

Photocopy this page onto card and cut into reading cards.
Store cards in an envelope and stick the label on the front for reference.
Can also be photocopied twice on different coloured card and cut into cards to make a simple matching game.

Book 6

Reading and spelling words with 'oo' spellings

oo	ou	ew
______	______	______
______	______	______
______	______	______
______	______	______
______	______	______

u	ue	u-e
______	______	______
______	______	______
______	______	______

soon group rude blew route truth proof
few super clues moon true grew soup
rule choose youth swoop threw blue July
you chew brute

List the words according to the 'oo' spellings.

Book 6

Timed reading of words with 'oo' spellings

grew   soon   you   blew   rude   too   soup
drew   true   brute   rule   cruel   foolish   super
flew   group   cool   swoop   youth   judo   threw
truly   include   gruesome   conclude   truth
choose   route   brew   flute   proof   plume

1st try   Time:

---

grew   soon   you   blew   rude   too   soup
drew   true   brute   rule   cruel   foolish   super
flew   group   cool   swoop   youth   judo   threw
truly   include   gruesome   conclude   truth
choose   route   brew   flute   proof   plume

2nd try   Time:

---

grew   soon   you   blew   rude   too   soup
drew   true   brute   rule   cruel   foolish   super
flew   group   cool   swoop   youth   judo   threw
truly   include   gruesome   conclude   truth
choose   route   brew   flute   proof   plume

3rd try   Time:

This timed reading exercise is for the pupil to improve his/her reading speed and fluency. Ask the pupil to read the words as fast as he/she can. Record the time in the box. Repeat the exercise. This sheet can be cut or folded along the dotted lines to allow for different presentations.

Book 6

Chunking two-syllable words with 'oo'

Word	Syllable 1	Syllable 2	Whole word
bamboo	bam	boo	bamboo
youthful			
chewing			
clueless			
include			
snooker			
coupon			
brutal			
gruesome			
intrude			
tattoo			
salute			
truthful			
stooping			

Split the word into two syllables. Write each syllable in a box.
Write the whole word while saying the syllables.

Book 6

Phonic patterns

Colour in the words with 'oo' spellings.

blue	group	flute	hoop
soup	rotten	balloon	shopping
coupon	toad	stoop	chew
limping	spray	explain	band
conclude	shampoo	rule	jewel

Fold this sheet on the dotted line. Read the words in the column on the left. Listen to the sounds in the words. Colour in the lozenges with words that have 'oo' spellings. Repeat this in the other columns. Unfold the sheet and check the correct words have been coloured in.

Is it true?

Jack and Ash wake up feeling really happy. They find a tin of food under a tree. Ash tells a story about some lost booty and Jack dreams about buying a plane. They scatter pebbles under the trees to help them find their way. The rain washes the pebbles away. Luckily Jack spots a tent in the distance that they can shelter in.

There are **5** things in the story above that are not true. Can you spot them?

Ask the pupil to read the text carefully and circle any false information
that has been planted in the story.

Book 6

Picture the scene

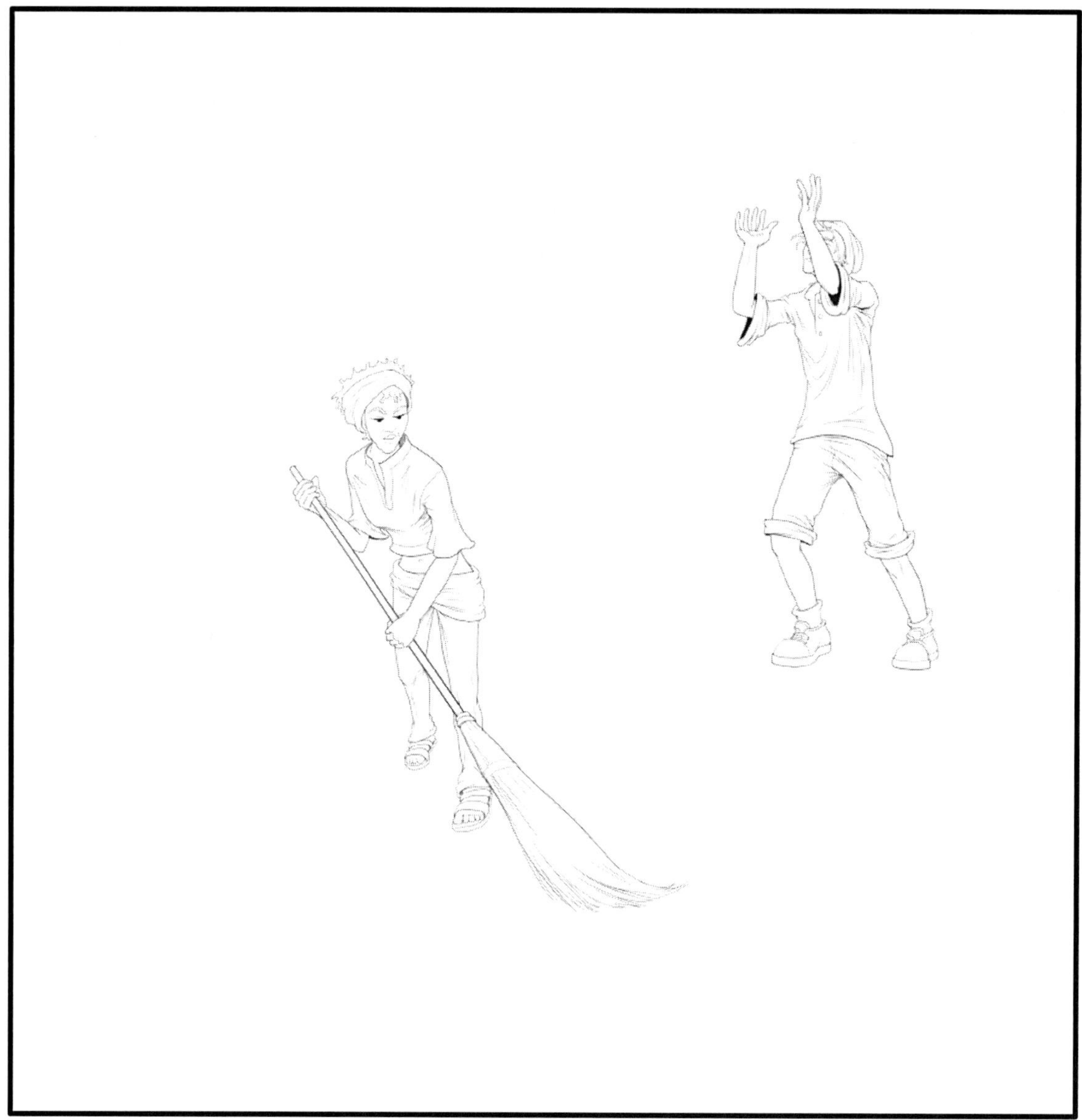

Jack is standing on a bed.

Ash is sweeping a rug.

There is a table on the left-hand side of Ash.

The table has a jug on it.

There is a round lampshade hanging from the ceiling between Jack and Ash.

Ask the pupil to read the text carefully and draw the details of the picture as described in the text.
Encourage them to read through all the text carefully before they begin working so they can plan their drawing.

Book 6

Dictation

Jack rested back on the ground.

"Are there any __ __ ___ __ about where it's hidden?" he said.

He began to daydream about the best way to spend all those

___ __ ___ __ of gold.

"I think we have to __ __ __ __ out hunting for gold today," said

Ash __ ___ __ __ ___ __. "We are as lost as that chest of

__ ___ __ __ _ is. Stop __ __ ___ __ __ ___. We need to find

your gran and Danny."

A massive rock __ ___ __ ___ over them in the forest.

"If we get to the top of that we'll be able to see all the forest."

Jack rested back on the ground.

"Are there any **c l ue s** about where it's hidden?" he said.

He began to daydream about the best way to send all those **oo d le s** of gold.

"I think we have to **r u l e** out hunting for gold today," said Ash **r ue f u ll y**. "We are as lost as that chest of **j ew e l s** is. Stop **s n oo z i ng**. We need to find your gran and Danny.

A massive rock **l oo m ed** over them in the forest.

"If we get to the top of that we'll be able to see all the forest."

Use the text at the bottom of the page for dictation. The section for dictation can either be cut off by the teacher or folded along the dotted line to allow the pupil to self-check their spellings on completion.
Dictate the passage to the pupil. Ask them to spell the missing words, writing a sound on each line. Explain that a longer line indicates a spelling with more than one letter e.g. l oo m ed

Book 6

Punctuation exercise

Speech marks, question marks and full stops

Jack rested back on the ground

Are there any clues about where it's hidden

he said He began to daydream about the best

way to spend all those oodles of gold

There is a set of speech marks, a question mark and 3 full stops missing from the text above.

Did you spot them all?

Ask the pupil to read through the text and add in speech marks, a question mark and full stops where necessary. Encourage the pupil to read aloud as this will help him/her identify where the punctuation occurs.

Book 6

Developing vocabulary: **snoozing**

The word 'snoozing' is used here in Book 6:

> "We are as lost as that chest of jewels is. Stop **snoozing**. We need to find your gran and Danny."

'Snoozing' is another word for sleeping or napping.

Circle the word or phrase that could be replaced with the word 'snoozing' in the following text:

> It was warm and cosy in the old barn. The cats were sleeping happily on the old sofa.

Can you write two different sentences of your own using the word 'snoozing'?

1.

____

____

2.

____

____

Book 6

Retell the story

Use the pictures below to retell the story in Book 6.

Photocopy the pictures above onto card and cut them out. Jumble them up and ask the pupil to sequence and number them in the correct order of the story. Ask the pupil to retell the story in his/her own words. Then ask the pupil to write the story on a separate sheet of paper.

Book 6: Stepping stones reading game: 'oo' words

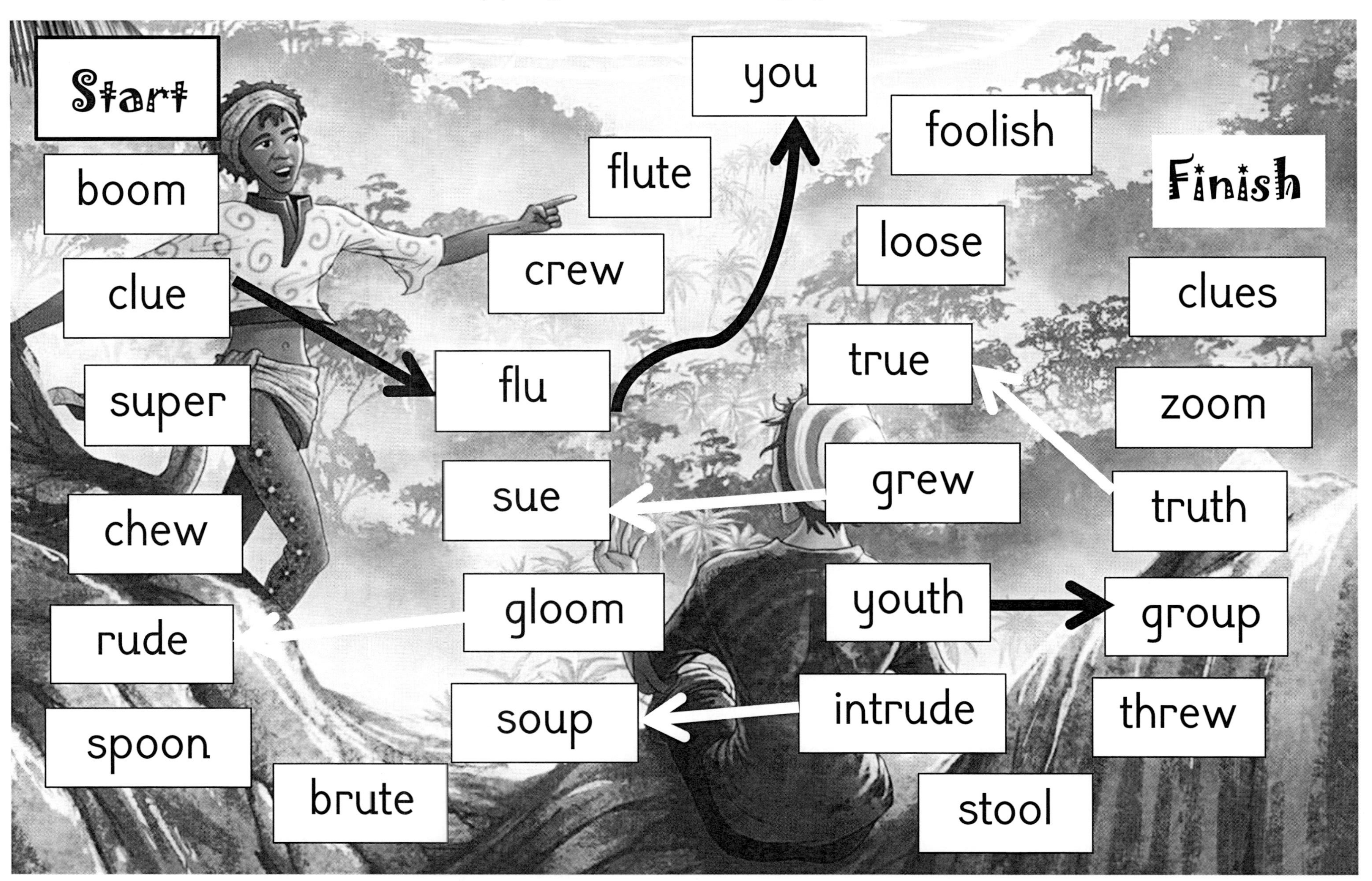

A game for 1–4 players: Play with counters and dice.
Players should read aloud the words that they land on at the end of each turn and follow the black and white direction arrows if they land on them.

This sheet may be photocopied by the purchaser. © Phonic Books Ltd 2019

Book 6

Non fiction:

Mountain apples – Bullet points

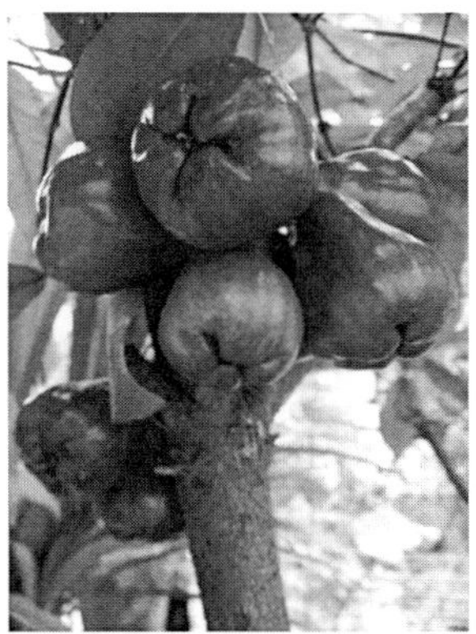

Mountain apples are also known as Malay apples. The trees are very tall and can grow to 50 or 60 feet. Many apples can grow on a tree. The trees are tropical and need a hot climate to grow. The apples can be longer than normal apples and are shaped a little like a pear. They are usually rose-coloured with a smooth, waxy skin and crisp white flesh. Mountain apples do not taste the same as other apples. They have a mild, sweet flavour. They can taste a little bland when raw but are tastier when stewed. Some varieties have a white skin.

Mountain Apples

1.

2.

3.

4.

5.

6.

This sheet provides the information needed to make an information card about mountain apples. Ask the pupil to read the text carefully and condense the information to make 6 bullet points about mountain apples. They can then use this information to create the card in the box below.

Dice game: words with 'oo' spellings

you	blew	loot	boom	clue	drew
rude	flu	flute	brew	true	stoop
noon	super	soup	blue	rule	route
loose	group	brutal	jewel	gloom	loop
grew	judo	prune	glue	threw	truth

This game is for two players. Each player needs a batch of counters of one colour. The players take turns to throw the die. They read a word in the column that corresponds to the number on the die and place their counter on that word. The first to have three of his/her counters in a row in any direction is the winner.

Book 6

Spelling assessment for words with 'oo' spellings

1.

oo	ou	ew	u	ue	u–e
too	you	new	flu	blue	rude
soon	soup	flew	ruler	glue	rule
food	group	grew	super	true	flute

2.

oo	ou	ew	u	ue	u–e
broom	youthful	threw	brutal	cruel	rudely
foolish	grouping	stewing	truthful	gruesome	intrude

These lists can be used as a spelling assessment at the end of each book. The teacher can add words from list 2 for pupils who are ready for that stage. When dictating a word, first say the word on its own. Next, say a sentence with the word in it (to put the word in the context of a sentence) and then repeat the word. This ensures that the pupil has heard the word correctly, e.g. "New. The boy loved his new jumper. New."

Island Adventure Series
Book 7: An Amazing Find

Contents

Book 7
Blending and segmenting: 'ie'

right	r	igh	t		
tie	☐	☐			
line	☐	i	☐	e	
my	☐	☐			
mind	☐	☐	☐	☐	
style	☐	☐	☐	☐	
drive	☐	☐	☐	☐	☐
final	☐	☐	☐	☐	☐
shine	☐	☐	☐	☐	
tonight	☐	☐	☐	☐	☐
slimy	☐	☐	☐	☐	☐
applied	☐	☐	☐	☐	☐
tighten	☐	☐	☐	☐	☐

Blend the sounds into a word. Segment the word into sounds by writing one sound in each square.
Split vowel spellings (i–e) are represented by half squares linked together.

Book 7
Reading and sorting words with 'ie' spellings

| igh | ie | i–e | i | y |

giant	idol	midnight	flies
shy	thigh	slime	invite
final	try	mine	high
life	dried	kite	slight
find	line	why	die
kind	dive	spies	nice
bright	lying	behind	fright
knife	shine	style	Book 7 Reading cards 'ie' spellings

Photocopy this page onto card and cut into reading cards.
Store cards in an envelope and stick the label on the front for reference.
Can also be photocopied twice on different coloured card and cut into cards to make a simple matching game.

Book 7

Reading and spelling words with 'ie' spellings

igh	ie	i–e
_____	_____	_____
_____	_____	_____
_____	_____	_____
_____	_____	_____
_____	_____	_____

i	y
_____	_____
_____	_____
_____	_____

right slight frighten pie fried mine cried
lies fine bright shine write final tonight die
I'm try white by I why

List the words according to the 'ie' spellings.

Book 7

Timed reading of words with 'ie' spellings

final   try   mine   high   life   dried   kite   slight
find   life   why   die   kind   dive   spies   nice
bright   lying   behind   fright   knife   shine   mile
style   giant   idol   midnight   flies   shy   thigh
slime   invite   tighten   rice

1st try   Time:

---

final   try   mine   high   life   dried   kite   slight
find   life   why   die   kind   dive   spies   nice
bright   lying   behind   fright   knife   shine   mile
style   giant   idol   midnight   flies   shy   thigh
slime   invite   tighten   rice

2nd try   Time:

---

final   try   mine   high   life   dried   kite   slight
find   life   why   die   kind   dive   spies   nice
bright   lying   behind   fright   knife   shine   mile
style   giant   idol   midnight   flies   shy   thigh
slime   invite   tighten   rice

3rd try   Time:

This timed reading exercise is for the pupil to improve his/her reading speed and fluency. Ask the pupil to read the words as fast as he/she can. Record the time in the box. Repeat the exercise. This sheet can be cut or folded along the dotted lines to allow for different presentations.

Book 7

Chunking two-syllable words with 'ie'

sunlight	sun	light	sunlight
inside			
slimy			
magpie			
spicy			
reply			
dryer			
decide			
title			
denied			
delight			
beside			
refried			
stylish			

Split the word into two syllables. Write each syllable in a box.
Write the whole word while saying the syllables.

Book 7

Phonic patterns

Colour in the words with 'ie' spellings.

flight	inside	still	timeless
crying	hippo	twins	spilled
might	knight	dye	write
shipment	mile	brick	brighten
hyper	blind	cringe	flight

Fold this sheet on the dotted line. Read the words in the column on the left. Listen to the sounds in the words. Colour in the lozenges with words that have 'ie' spellings. Repeat this in the other columns. Unfold the sheet and check the correct words have been coloured in.

Is it true?

Ash and Jack wake up in the old tent.
They find a piece of paper under the bed.
The map shows a red cross in the middle
of the town. They follow the map and
discover some amazing frogs! They still
need to find Gran and Danny. They
explore a cave and find a bag full of
cakes. They write a message on the beach
with bottle tops.

There are **6** things in the story above that are
not true. Can you spot them?

Ask the pupil to read the text carefully and circle any false information that has been
planted in the story.

Book 7

Picture the scene

Ash and Jack are holding a map.

There is a big cross in the middle of the map.

There is a lamp behind the map.

The lamp is on top of a table.

There is a jug on the table too.

Ask the pupil to read the text carefully and draw the details of the picture as described in the text. Encourage them to read through all the text carefully before they begin working so they can plan their drawing.

Book 7

Dictation

Ash woke up at first __ ____ __. Jack had found a ____ __ __ __

and was cutting up __ __ __ __ apples.

"Apples for breakfast ... with a __ __ __ __ dish of apples!" he joked.

"Just apples?" I wish it was __ __ __ __ __ __ of __ __ __ __

hot apple __ ____ with cream!" groaned Ash.

The house had been empty for a long __ __ __ __. There was

not much left __ __ __ __ __ __ it.

Jack found a __ ____ __ __ __ folded note hidden on a __ ____

shelf. Was it a map? It __ ____ __ help them __ __ __ __

that chest of gold.

Ash woke up at first **l igh t**. Jack had found a **kn i f e** and was cutting up **r i p e** apples.

"Apples for breakfast ... with a **s i d e** dish of apples!" he joked.

"Just apples?" I wish it was **s l i c e s** of **n i c e** hot apple **p ie** with cream!" groaned Ash.

The house had been empty for a long **t i m e**. There was not much left **i n s i d e** it. Jack found a **t igh t l y**

folded note hidden on a **h igh** shelf. Was it a map? It **m igh t** help them **f i n d** that chest of gold.

Use the text at the bottom of the page for dictation. The section for dictation can either be cut off by the teacher or folded along the dotted line to allow the pupil to self-check their spellings on completion. Dictate the passage to the pupil. Ask them to spell the missing words, writing a sound on each line.
Explain that a longer line indicates a spelling with more than one letter e.g. l igh t.

Book 7

Punctuation exercise

Speech marks and exclamation marks

It's blank, said Jack with a shrug. Not exactly a prize find. Just a bit of rubbish.

A sudden breeze from the open window snatched the paper. It blew right up against the lamp.

Look at the paper Ash cried out. It has writing on it

There are 4 sets of speech marks and 2 exclamation marks missing.

Did you spot them all?

Ask the pupil to read through the text and add in speech marks and exclamation marks where necessary. Remind the pupil that exclamation marks are often used when there is surprise or excitement.

Book 7

Developing vocabulary: **bobbed**

The word 'bobbed' is used here in Book 7:

> Dark shadows bobbed under the waves. She had a sudden fright. What was hiding in the sea?

'Bobbed' is another word for moved up and down quickly. It is used here to describe the movement of the turtles under the water.

Circle the word or phrase that could be replaced with the word 'bobbed' in the following text:

> The old man was so excited. His head jerked up and down. "Yes!" he yelled. "Yes, please!"

Can you write two different sentences of your own using the word 'bobbed'?

1.

____

____

2.

____

____

Book 7

Retell the story

Use the pictures below to retell the story in Book 7.

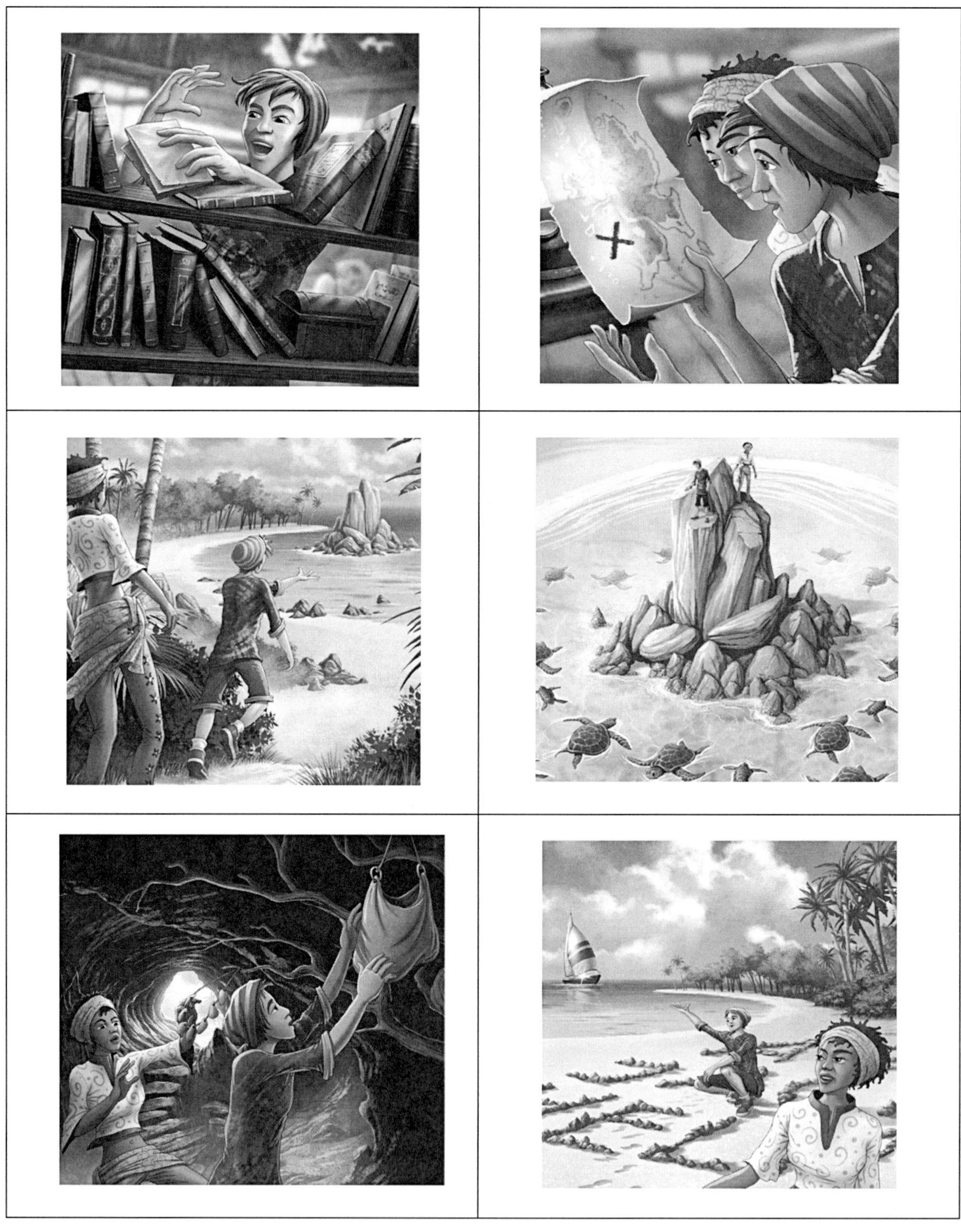

Photocopy the pictures above onto card and cut them out. Jumble them up and ask the pupil to sequence and number them in the correct order of the story. Ask the pupil to retell the story in his/her own words. Then ask the pupil to write the story on a separate sheet of paper.

Book 7: Stepping stones reading game: 'ie' words

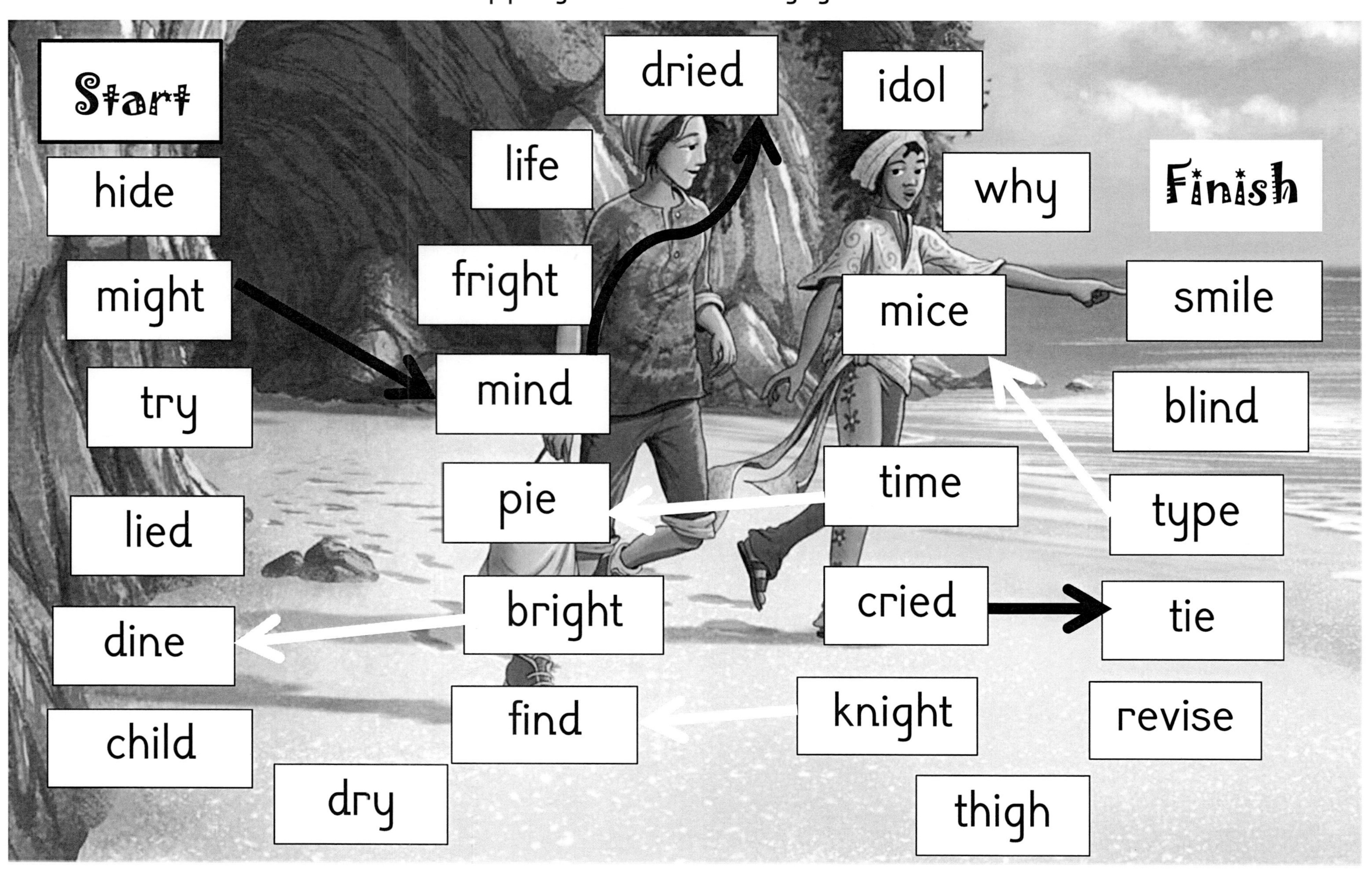

A game for 1–4 players: Play with counters and dice.

Players should read aloud the words that they land on at the end of each turn and follow the black and white direction arrows if they land on them.

This sheet may be photocopied by the purchaser. © Phonic Books Ltd 2019

Book 7

Non fiction: Secret messages

Jack and Ash discover a secret map on a piece of paper when the paper blows up against a lamp. The heat reveals the message. This is fun but can be dangerous as the paper could burn. A safer way of writing a secret message to someone is to use a secret code. There are many different types of these. Here are two different ways to try:

Writing words backwards

> ## Hello. What is your name?
> ## ?eman ruoy si tahW .olleH

Write the message backwards one letter at a time.

Start on the right-hand side of the page and write each letter one at a time. Remember to leave breaks when you write a new word.

Add any punctuation, like capital letters and full stops, at the end.

Writing the alphabet backwards

A	B	C	D	E	F	G	H	I	J	K	L	M	N	O	P	Q	R	S	T	U	V	W	X	Y	Z
z	y	x	w	v	u	t	s	r	q	p	o	n	m	l	k	j	i	h	g	f	e	d	c	b	a

hello friend   svool uirvmw

Write out the entire alphabet neatly, giving plenty of space to write directly below it. Write it in one long row along the long side of a piece of paper

After you've written it out in normal order, then write it in reversed order. Write the reversed alphabet directly underneath the first alphabet so each letter matches one above it. This means that z will sit under A, y under B, x under C, and so on.

Write your message using the letters from the bottom row of the alphabet.

This sheet provides the information needed to write a message with a secret code. Ask the pupil to choose one of the codes to write their message. They can then see if someone else can crack their code and read the message.

Dice game: words with 'ie' spellings

1	2	3	4	5	6
lime	my	high	kite	lie	try
rind	fright	spy	why	bike	fight
fry	five	cried	final	shy	tight
hide	strike	China	reply	drive	slight
dried	bite	sky	revise	spine	pipe

This game is for two players. Each player needs a batch of counters of one colour. The players take turns to throw the die. They read a word in the column that corresponds to the number on the die and place their counter on that word. The first to have three of his/her counters in a row in any direction is the winner.

Book 7

Spelling assessment for words with 'ie' spellings

1.	**igh**	**ie**	**i-e**	**i**	**y**
	right	tie	time	I	my
	light	die	like	mind	by
	might	pie	pipe	find	try

2.	**igh**	**ie**	**i-e**	**i**	**y**
	flight	cried	spike	grind	why
	tonight	spied	white	behind	reply

These lists can be used as a spelling assessment at the end of each book. The teacher can add words from list 2 for pupils who are ready for that stage. When dictating a word, first say the word on its own. Next, say a sentence with the word in it (to put the word in the context of a sentence) and then repeat the word. This ensures that the pupil has heard the word correctly, e.g. "Might. I might have chips for tea. Might."

Island Adventure Series
Book 8: Awesome Morning

Contents

Book 8
Blending and segmenting: 'or'

saw	s	aw
more		
all		
for		
war		

haunt				

fought			
walk			
torch			

before				
small				
straw				
swarm				

Blend the sounds into a word. Segment the word into sounds by writing one sound in each square.

Book 8
Reading and sorting words with 'or' spellings

Photocopy this page onto card and cut into reading cards.
Store cards in an envelope and stick the label on the front for reference.
Can also be photocopied twice on different coloured card and cut into cards to make a simple matching game.

Book 8

Reading and spelling words with 'or' spellings

or	**ore**	**a**

aw	**au**	**ar**

al	**ough**	**awe**

or   thought   call   more   before   saw   August   warm
awe   walk   fought   torch   store   all   almost   draw
haunt   war   brought   stalk   awesome   nought   snore
small   claw   assault   swarm   talk   born   Autumn
reward   awful   for

List the words according to the 'or' spellings.

Book 8

Timed reading of words with 'or' spellings

snore sport awful talk for bore tall wart
fought Paul halt awesome born store call
warm haunt thought stalk draw stork tore
almost swarm walk August claw nought
morning explore stall paw

1st try   **Time:**

---

snore sport awful talk for bore tall wart
fought Paul halt awesome born store call
warm haunt thought stalk draw stork tore
almost swarm walk August claw nought
morning explore stall paw

2nd try   **Time:**

---

snore sport awful talk for bore tall wart
fought Paul halt awesome born store call
warm haunt thought stalk draw stork tore
almost swarm walk August claw nought
morning explore stall paw

3rd try   **Time:**

This timed reading exercise is for the pupil to improve his/her reading speed and fluency. Ask the pupil to read the words as fast as he/she can. Record the time in the box. Repeat the exercise. This sheet can be cut or folded along the dotted lines to allow for different presentations.

Book 8

Chunking two-syllable words with 'or'

before	be	fore	before
morning			
almost			
awful			
haunted			
warming			
thoughtful			
talking			
sorted			
boredom			
calling			
August			
lawless			
report			

Split the word into two syllables. Write each syllable in a box.
Write the whole word while saying the syllables.

Book 8

Phonic patterns

Colour in the words with 'or' spellings.

poppy	corn	bore	warm
talk	hungry	bangle	shallow
torch	fatten	warm	saw
landing	short	crawl	band
torn	stall	awesome	report

Fold this sheet on the dotted line. Read the words in the column on the left. Listen to the sounds in the words. Colour in the lozenges with words that have 'or' spellings. Repeat this in the other columns. Unfold the sheet and check the correct words have been coloured in.

This sheet may be photocopied by the purchaser. © Phonic Books Ltd 2019

Is it true?

Ash and Jack are rescued when Gran and Danny arrive in a plane. They set off back to Danny's camp. Gran has discovered some tiny parrots in the forest. Jack falls off a bridge. He lands in a web and is frightened by four huge spiders. Ash uses her shoelaces to rescue Jack. Danny cooks them soup on the beach.

There are **6** things in the story above that are not true. Can you spot them?

Ask the pupil to read the text carefully and circle any false information
that has been planted in the story.

Book 8

Picture the scene

There are two tall trees at the edge of
the picture.

A huge spider's web is stretched between
the trees.

There are three spiders on the web.

The moon is in the sky above the web.

Jack is running on a carpet of leaves.

Ask the pupil to read the text carefully and draw the details of the picture as described in the text.
Encourage them to read through all the text carefully before they begin working so they can plan
their drawing.

Book 8

Dictation

Suddenly Ash jumped in fright.

"There are __ __ ___ __ __ of frogs on my feet," she yelled.

"___ __ __ ___." grinned Jack.

"The frogs are __ ___ __ ___ ___ an __ ___ ___ __ __!"

They took masses of film of the frogs. By suppertime it was still __ __ ___ ___ ___ hot and Jack was starting to __ ___ __

with __ ___ __ __ __.

"Go and __ __ __ __ ___," Gran told him. "A ___ ___ __

__ ___ __ will stretch __ ___ legs __ __ __ ___ we stop

and eat.

Suddenly Ash jumped I fright.

"There are **s w ar m s** of frogs on my feet," she yelled.

"**Awe s o me,** " grinned Jack. "The frogs are **l au n ch ing** an **a ss au l t** !"

They took masses of films of the frogs. By suppertime it was still **s c or ch ing** hot and Jack was starting to **y aw n** with **b ore d o m**.

"Go and **e x p l ore**," Gran told him. "A **sh or t w al k** will stretch **y our** legs **b e f ore** we stop and eat.

Use the text at the bottom of the page for dictation. The section for dictation can either be cut off by the teacher or folded along the dotted line to allow the pupil to self-check their spellings on completion. Dictate the passage to the pupil. Ask them to spell the missing words, writing a sound on each line.
Explain that a longer line indicates a spelling with more than one letter e.g. th ough t

Book 8

Punctuation exercise

Apostrophes and speech marks

Dont struggle, warned Ash. If you dont disturb them theyll ignore you.

Jack forced himself to stay calm. He used his free hand to claw his way out of the sticky web. The spiders swayed in the breeze but they didnt crawl towards him.

There are 4 apostrophes and 2 sets of speech marks missing.

Did you spot them all?

Ask the pupil to read through the text and add in apostrophes and speech where necessary. Explain that in this text apostrophes are used where two words have been combined and some letters are missing. The apostrophes replace these letters.

Book 8

Developing vocabulary: **hurling**

The word 'hurling' is used here in Book 8:

A big chunk of the log broke off, **hurling** Jack down into a deep pit.

'Hurling' is another word for

throwing with great strength.

Circle the word or phrase that could be replaced with the word 'hurling' in the following text:

The twins had made up a competition. They were both throwing pebbles into the sea to see which one would go the furthest.

Can you write two different sentences of your own using the word 'hurling'?

1.

____

____

2.

____

____

Book 8

Retell the story

Use the pictures below to retell the story in Book 8.

Photocopy the pictures above onto card and cut them out. Jumble them up and ask the pupil to sequence and number them in the correct order of the story. Ask the pupil to retell the story in his/her own words. Then ask the pupil to write the story on a separate sheet of paper.

Book 8: Stepping stones reading game: 'or' words

Start

Finish

explore

bore

call

wart

fought

halt

nought

thought

haunt

warm

morning

store

born

stalk

draw

paw

tore

almost

swarm

walk

tall

stork

for

awe

claw

August

A game for 1–4 players: Play with counters and dice.
Players should read aloud the words that they land on at the end of each turn and follow the black and white direction arrows if they land on them.

This sheet may be photocopied by the purchaser. © Phonic Books Ltd 2019

Book 8

Non fiction:

Giant spiders' web – Newspaper report

A Greek beach has been covered in a spiders' web more than 300 metres long.

The beach in western Greece was discovered by fishermen in the early hours of Wednesday morning. Trees and bushes along the beach were under siege from the dense web.

The web was built by Tetragnatha spiders, often known as stretch spiders. Stretch spiders have elongated bodies. They are small enough and light enough to be able to run across water. They can run faster on water than they can move on land.

Luckily, the spiders are not dangerous and don't pose a threat to humans.

"These spiders are not dangerous and will not cause any harm," molecular biologist Giorgos Papadaki told Greek news websites. He explained that the phenomenon can occur when the spiders are mating, and that an increase in the mosquito population this year had created perfect conditions for a population explosion among the spiders.

"The spiders are taking advantage of these conditions, and are having a kind of web party".

He noted that the phenomenon had previously been seen before in the region, in 2003, and that the spiders would soon die off, and the web would degrade naturally, leaving the vegetation undamaged.

Boy trapped in giant spiders' web!

This sheet provides the information needed to write a newspaper report about Jack being caught in a giant spiders' web. Ask the pupil to read the text carefully, noting the style it is written in and seeing any factual information that will be useful to make their report. They should then write a report about what happened to Jack.

Book 8

Dice game: words with 'or' spellings

(1)	(2)	(3)	(4)	(5)	(6)
ball	warn	score	corn	core	prawn
walk	sport	more	stall	bore	fault
claw	war	fought	awe	lawn	torn
sore	small	haunt	draw	stork	awful
halt	shore	horse	hall	talk	dawn

This game is for two players. Each player needs a batch of counters of one colour. The players take turns to throw the die. They read a word in the column that corresponds to the number on the die and place their counter on that word. The first to have three of his/her counters in a row in any direction is the winner.

Book 8

Spelling assessment for words with 'or' spellings

or	**ore**	**aw**	**au**	**al**
or	more	saw	August	talk
for	store	draw	Autumn	walks
morning	before	prawn	author	stalk

ar	**awe**	**a**	**ough**
war	awe	all	fought
warm	awesome	small	thought
swarm		almost	brought

These lists can be used as a spelling assessment at the end of each book. The teacher may want to offer this test in two halves as there are so may spellings. When dictating a word, first say the word on its own. Next, say a sentence with the word in it (to put the word in the context of a sentence) and then repeat the word. This ensures that the pupil has heard the word correctly, e.g. "Warm. It was warm in the sun. Warm."

Island Adventure Series
Book 9: Don't Be Scared

Contents

Book 9
Blending and segmenting: 'air'

pair	p	air				
care						
their						
bear						
chair						
share						
where						
swear						
stair						
spare						
beware						
careless						
werewolf						

Blend the sounds into a word. Segment the word into sounds by writing one sound in each square.

Book 9
Reading and sorting words with 'air' spellings

air	**are**	**ear**	**ere**	**eir**

fair	chair	wear	bear
pair	swear	stare	there
blare	mare	tear	dare
wear	flair	bare	pear
there	their	fair	declare
heir	affair	stair	compare
spare	care	rare	fairly
stare	glare	flare	Book 9 Reading cards 'air' spellings

Photocopy this page onto card and cut into reading cards.
Store cards in an envelope and stick the label on the front for reference.
Can also be photocopied twice on different coloured card and cut into cards to
make a simple matching game.

Book 9

Reading and spelling words with 'air' spellings

air	are	ear
_________	_________	_________
_________	_________	_________
_________	_________	_________
_________	_________	_________
_________	_________	
_________	_________	
_________	_________	

ere	eir
_________	_________
_________	_________

aware   their   bear   there   chair   care   swear
fare   tear   repair   hair   glare   fair   dairy   pear
share   airport   air   spare   where   scare   heir

List the words according to the 'air' spellings.

Book 9

Timed reading of words with 'air' spellings

air   there   scare   chair   their   pear   tear
where   hair   theirs   repair   lair   share   dairy
bear   fair   declare   fare   swear   aware   wear
warehouse   beware   fairly   stare   fair   bear
mare   care   repair   compare

1st try   Time:

---

air   there   scare   chair   their   pear   tear
where   hair   theirs   repair   lair   share   dairy
bear   fair   declare   fare   swear   aware   wear
warehouse   beware   fairly   stare   fair   bear
mare   care   repair   compare

2nd try   Time:

---

air   there   scare   chair   their   pear   tear
where   hair   theirs   repair   lair   share   dairy
bear   fair   declare   fare   swear   aware   wear
warehouse   beware   fairly   stare   fair   bear
mare   care   repair   compare

3rd try   Time:

This timed reading exercise is for the pupil to improve his/her reading speed and fluency. Ask the pupil to read the words as fast as he/she can. Record the time in the box. Repeat the exercise. This sheet can be cut or folded along the dotted lines to allow for different presentations.

Book 9

Chunking two-syllable words with 'air'

hairless	*hair*	*less*	*hairless*
unfair			
footwear			
declare			
repair			
heirloom			
rarely			
careless			
affair			
despair			
farewell			
nowhere			
beware			
compare			

Split the word into two syllables. Write each syllable in a box.
Write the whole word while saying the syllables.

Book 9

Phonic patterns

Colour in the words with 'air' spellings.

ready	dare	helpful	there
scare	runner	fitted	pain
where	share	made	pair
fate	theirs	barely	stampede
glare	green	affair	rare

Fold this sheet on the dotted line. Read the words in the column on the left. Listen to the sounds in the words. Colour in the lozenges with words that have 'air' spellings. Repeat this in the other columns. Unfold the sheet and check the correct words have been coloured in.

Is it true?

Jack gets a fright when Gran wakes him up in the middle of the night! They go out to watch the penguins. On the way back home Ash is suddenly scared. She sees something in the shadows. She thinks it is a monster. Luckily it is just a large rock. Ash spots a damaged turtle. He has a very sore eye and his shell is covered in paint.

There are **5** things in the story above that are not true. Can you spot them?

Ask the pupil to read the text carefully and circle any false information
that has been planted in the story.

Book 9

Picture the scene

There is a beach in front of the characters,
with the beach in front of the sea.

There are six turtles on the sandy beach.

The moon is in the sky above Jack's head.

There are three palm trees on the beach.

Ask the pupil to read the text carefully and draw the details of the picture as described in the text.
Encourage them to read through all the text carefully before they begin working so they can plan
their drawing.

Book 9

Dictation

Moonlight shone like a torch across the sea.

Suddenly they were __ __ ___ of a stream of shapes plodding

__ ___ __ __ ___ __ across the sand.

"Take __ ___ not to be seen," murmured Danny. "We must stay

out of sight so we don't __ __ ___ them. If they feel safe they

will dig a pit with ___ ___ flippers and lay ___ ___ eggs.

They hid in the tall grass above the beach. Jack was hungry.

"I wish we had a snack to ___ ___," he moaned.

They stayed as still as stones, __ __ __ __ ___ __ for a

long wait.

Moonlight shone like a torch across the sea.

Suddenly they were **a w are** of a stream of shapes plodding **c are f u ll y** across the sand.

"Take **c are** not to be seen," murmured Danny. "We must stay out of sight so we don't **s c are**

them. If they feel safe they will dig a pit with **th eir** flippers and lay **th eir** eggs.

They hid in the tall grass above the beach. Jack was hungry.

"I wish we had a snack to **sh are**," he moaned.

They stayed as still as stones, **p r e p are d** for a long wait.

Use the text at the bottom of the page for dictation. The section for dictation can either be cut off by the teacher or folded along the dotted line to allow the pupil to self-check their spellings on completion. Dictate the passage to the pupil. Ask them to spell the missing words, writing a sound on each line.
Explain that a longer line indicates a spelling with more than one letter e.g. h eir.

Book 9

Punctuation exercise

All punctuation

dawn was breaking as they stumbled into camp i think her flipper has been snared in some wire sobbed ash she needs medical care right now where can we get help

All the punctuation is missing from the text above.

Can you put in 5 capital letter, 3 full stops,

2 sets of speech marks, 1 comma and 1 question mark?

Ask the pupil to read through the text and add in capital letters and punctuation where necessary. Encourage the pupil to read aloud as this will help him/her identify where the sentences stop.

Book 9

Developing vocabulary: **hared**

The word 'hared' is used here in Book 9:

Circle the word or phrase that could be replaced with the word 'hared' in the following text:

> Mick's eyes glinted. He loved races and always tried his best to win. As soon as he heard the whistle blow he ran along the track as fast as he could.

Can you write two different sentences of your own using the word 'hared'?

1.

____

____

2.

____

____

Book 9

Retell the story

Use the pictures below to retell the story in Book 9.

Photocopy the pictures above onto card and cut them out. Jumble them up and ask the pupil to sequence and number them in the correct order of the story. Ask the pupil to retell the story in his/her own words. Then ask the pupil to write the story on a separate sheet of paper.

Book 9: Stepping stones reading game: 'air' words

A game for 1–4 players: Play with counters and dice. Players should read aloud the words that they land on at the end of each turn and follow the white direction arrows if they land on them.

This sheet may be photocopied by the purchaser. © Phonic Books Ltd 2019

Book 9

Non fiction:

Turtle nesting ground – Warning sign

Female turtles nest, most often at night. The turtle crawls out of the ocean, pausing often as if carefully looking for a good nesting place. Sea turtles are generally slow and find it awkward to walk on land. Nesting can be exhausting work.

The turtle crawls to a dry part of the beach. She begins to brush away any loose sand with her flippers. She then constructs a "body pit" by digging with her flippers and twisting her body around. After the body pit is complete, she uses her rear flippers to dig a hole for the eggs. The egg cavity is shaped a little like a tear drop.

When the turtle has finished digging the egg chamber, she begins to lay her eggs. Two or three eggs drop out at a time. The average size of a clutch ranges from about 80 to 120 eggs, depending on the species. The eggs are flexible which means they don't break as they fall into the chamber. Nesting sea turtles can look as if they're crying, but really they are just secreting salt that builds up in their body.

A sea turtle is not likely to abandon nesting when she is laying her eggs, but some turtles will abandon the process if they feel they are in danger. For this reason, it is important that sea turtles are never disturbed during nesting.

Once all the eggs are in the chamber, the mother turtle uses her rear flippers to push sand over the top of the egg cavity. She packs the sand down over the top and uses her front flippers to refill the body pit and disguise the nest. The turtle throws sand in all directions, which makes it harder for predators to find the eggs.

After the nest is completely hidden, the female crawls back to the sea to rest. Once a turtle has left her nest, she never returns to tend it.

Sea turtles nesting ground

This sheet provides the information needed to write a warning sign for dog walkers on the beach.
Encourage pupils to use some of the information above to alert dog walkers to the turtle nests.
Remind them that not all the information above will be relevant for their sign.

Book 9

Dice game: words with 'air' spellings

●	●●	●●●	●●●●	●●●●●	●●●●●●
dare	air	repair	chair	wear	fair
hairy	care	bear	share	swear	blare
there	flair	hair	where	tear	rare
pear	glare	stare	their	stairs	scare
heir	pair	fare	lair	hare	dairy

This game is for two players. Each player needs a batch of counters of one colour. The players take turns to throw the die. They read a word in the column that corresponds to the number on the die and place their counter on that word. The first to have three of his/her counters in a row in any direction is the winner.

Book 9

Spelling assessment for words with 'air' spellings

1.

air	are	ear	ere	eir
air	care	bear	there	their
hair	bare	pear	where	
pairs	hare	wear		

2.

air	are	ear	ere
chair	share	tears	werewolf
unfair	scare	swear	whereabouts
despair	spares		

These lists can be used as a spelling assessment at the end of each book. The teacher can add words from list 2 for students who are ready for that stage. When dictating a word, first say the word on its own. Next, say a sentence with the word in it (to put the word in the context of a sentence) and then repeat the word. This ensures that the student has heard the word correctly, e.g. "Bear. The bear was hidden in the trees. Bear."

Island Adventure Series
Book 10: Arty Party

Contents

Book 10
Blending and segmenting: 'ar'

art	ar	t			
ask					
half					
laugh					
heart					
path					
hard					
calm					
shark					
alarm					
hearth					
faster					
draught					

Blend the sounds into a word. Segment the word into sounds by writing one sound in each square.

Book 10
Reading and sorting words with 'ar' spellings

ar	a	al	au	ear

The pronunciation of the spellings of the 'ar' sound on this page may vary according to regional accent.

almond	castle	last	heart
harsh	ask	laugh	raft
past	shark	palm	calm
faster	half	harm	draught
after	star	dark	calf
trance	aunt	dance	march
bark	cast	army	charm
sharp	hearth	shard	Book 10 Reading cards 'ar' spellings

Photocopy this page onto card and cut into reading cards.
Store cards in an envelope and stick the label on the front for reference.
Can also be photocopied twice on different coloured card and cut into cards to make a simple matching game.

Book 10

Reading and spelling words with 'ar' spellings

ar	a	al
______	______	______
______	______	______
______	______	______
______	______	______
______	______	______

au	ear
______	______
______	______
______	______

calm   hearth   aunt   car   start   path   half   calf
ask   can't   fast   laughter   heart   sparse   past
carpet   laugh   hearts   dart   almond   palm

List the words according to the 'ar' spellings.

Book 10

Timed reading of words with 'ar' spellings

car   ask   garden   half   fast   laugh   past   park
far   aunt   laughed   heart   path   after   faster
dark   craft   art   hard   palm   hearth   rather
laughter   halve   almond   arm   can't   carpet
pardon   sharp   gasp   start

1st try   **Time:**

- -

car   ask   garden   half   fast   laugh   past   park
far   aunt   laughed   heart   path   after   faster
dark   craft   art   hard   palm   hearth   rather
laughter   halve   almond   arm   can't   carpet
pardon   sharp   gasp   start

2nd try   **Time:**

- -

car   ask   garden   half   fast   laugh   past   park
far   aunt   laughed   heart   path   after   faster
dark   craft   art   hard   palm   hearth   rather
laughter   halve   almond   arm   can't   carpet
pardon   sharp   gasp   start

3rd try   **Time:**

This timed reading exercise is for the pupil to improve his/her reading speed and fluency. Ask the pupil to read the words as fast as he/she can. Record the time in the box. Repeat the exercise. This sheet can be cut or folded along the dotted lines to allow for different presentations.

Book 10

Chunking two-syllable words with 'ar'

darkness	dark	ness	darkness
artist			
harmful			
father			
laughter			
hearty			
plaster			
advance			
castle			
basket			
almond			
draughty			
craftsman			
basket			

Split the word into two syllables. Write each syllable in a box.
Write the whole word while saying the syllables.

Book 10

Phonic patterns

Colour in the words with 'ar' spellings.

band	garden	clasp	snails
heart	lamp	pattern	bleak
sharp	battle	sparkle	darkness
sandpit	park	explain	speech
starving	great	mark	cartoon

Fold this sheet on the dotted line. Read the words in the column on the left. Listen to the sounds in the words. Colour in the lozenges with words that have 'ar' spellings. Repeat this in the other columns. Unfold the sheet and check the correct words have been coloured in.

Is it true?

They take the turtle to the clinic. The vet fixes the turtle's shell with sticky tape. It's time to leave the island. Jack, Ash and Gran get a ship home. Back home Gran is busy making her film. She launches the film at a cinema in the city. Mack, Ash and Danny can't make it to the party. Mack makes a stone statue of Jack and Ash with the turtles. They all watch the film in the sunrise.

There are **5** things in the story above that are not true. Can you spot them?

Ask the pupil to read the text carefully and circle any false information
that has been planted in the story.

Book 10

Picture the scene

There is a big screen between Gran and Jack and Snub.

Gran's new workshop is behind her.

There is a small bridge in front of Jack and Snub, crossing the gap between the two cliffs.

Waves are crashing against the bottom of the cliffs.

Ask the pupil to read the text carefully and draw the details of the picture as described in the text. Encourage them to read through all the text carefully before they begin working so they can plan their drawing.

Book 10

Dictation

It was getting ___ ____ __. Grandpa hung

__ __ ____ __ __ __ ____ fairy lights outside Gran's new

workshop. "It's a bit further inland this time," he joked. "We don't

want it falling into the sea again."

They were __ __ ____ __ ____ __ by a sudden loud roar. It

came from the sea. Jack jumped in __ __ ____ __. What was it?

Jack and Snub ran down to the edge of the sea.

It was __ ____ __ to see what was making the noise.

Jack __ __ __ __ __ ____ Snub's hand.

"Let's take the __ __ __ __!" he told her. "We won't go __ ____."

It was getting **d ar k**. Grandpa hung **s p ar k l i ng** fairy lights outside Gran's new workshop.

"It's a bit further inland this time," he joked. "We don't want it falling into the sea again."

They were **s t ar t le d** by a sudden loud roar. It came from the sea. Jack jumped in **a l ar m**.

What was it?

Jack and Snub ran down to the edge of the sea. It was **h ar d** to see what was making the noise.
Jack **g r a s p ed** Snub's hand.

"Let's take the **r a f t**!" he told her. "We won't go **f ar**."

Use the text at the bottom of the page for dictation. The section for dictation can either be cut off by the teacher or folded along the dotted line to allow the pupil to self-check their spellings on completion. Dictate the passage to the pupil. Ask them to spell the missing words, writing a sound on each line.
Explain that a longer line indicates a spelling with more than one letter e.g h ar m.

Book 10

Punctuation exercise

All punctation

the next day was their last day on the island

danny dropped them off at the airport

come back soon he told them

ash took a last look at the palm trees blowing in the wind

just try and stop us she laughed

All the punctuation is missing from the text above.

Can you put in 5 capital letter, 5 full stops,

2 sets of speech marks, 1 comma and 1 exclamation mark?

Ask the pupil to read through the text and add in capital letters and punctuation where necessary.
Encourage the pupil to read aloud as this will help him/her identify where the sentences stop.

Book 10

Developing vocabulary: **lurched**

The word 'lurched' is used here in Book 10:

'Lurched' is another word for suddenly tipping or rolling to one side.

Circle the word or phrase that could be replaced with the word 'lurched' in the following text:

A huge, icy wave hit the surfboard. Jenny clung on as the board rocked and tipped underneath her.

Can you write two different sentences of your own using the word 'lurched'?

1.

____

____

2.

____

____

Book 10

Retell the story

Use the pictures below to retell the story in Book 10.

Photocopy the pictures above onto card and cut them out. Jumble them up and ask the pupil to sequence and number them in the correct order of the story. Ask the pupil to retell the story in his/her own words. Then ask the pupil to write the story on a separate sheet of paper.

Book 10: Stepping stones reading game: 'ar' words

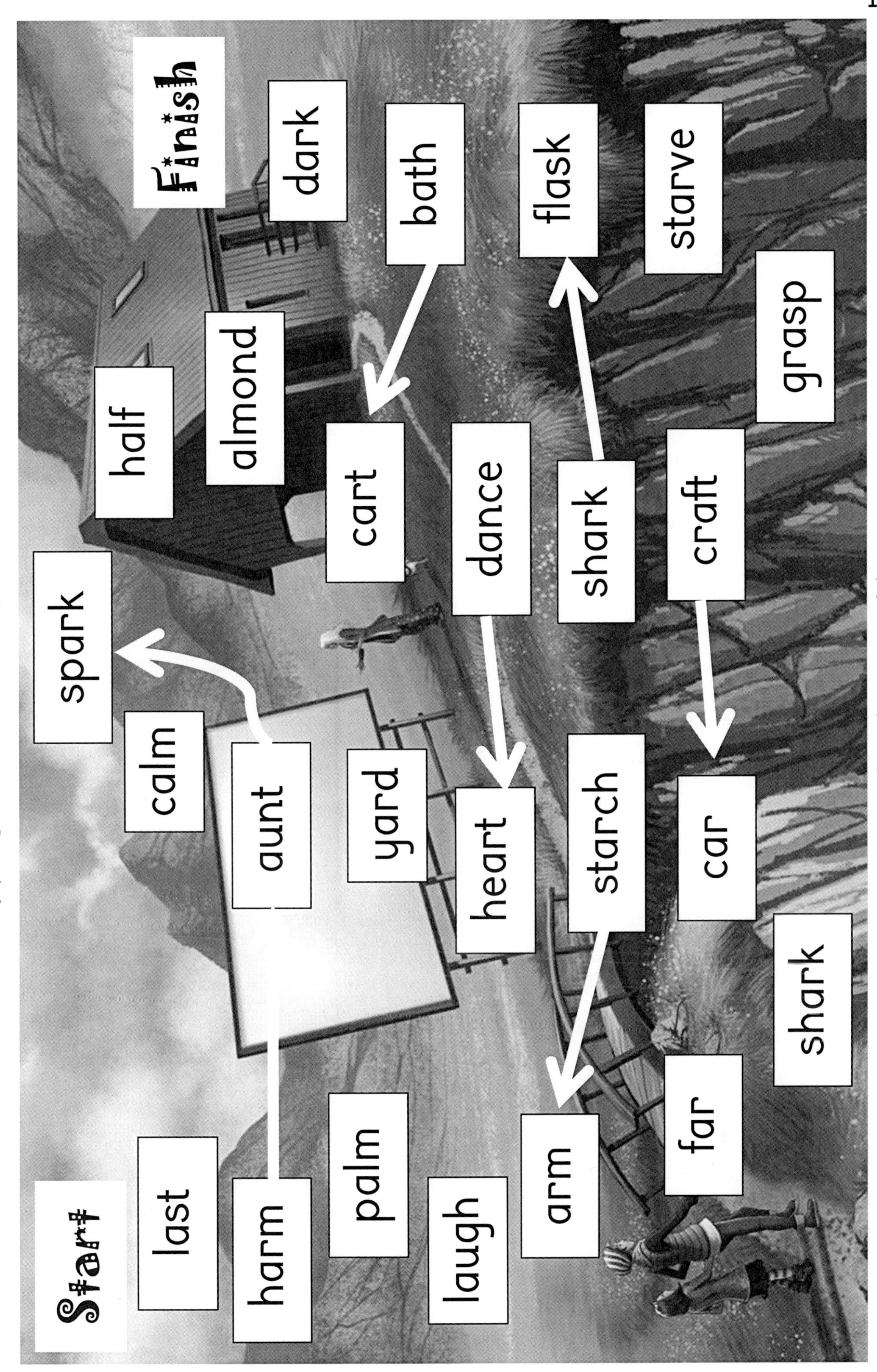

A game for 1–4 players: Play with counters and dice.
Players should read aloud the words that they land on at the end of each turn and follow the white direction arrows if they land on them.

This sheet may be photocopied by the purchaser. © Phonic Books Ltd 2019

Book 10

Non fiction:

Donated clasps to repair turtle shells – Flyer

A cracked shell is a serious health problem for sea turtles. Even minor cracks may lead to long–term health problems or infection. The shell cannot be left cracked. It must be repaired before a turtle can be released back into the wild. Unlike when a human breaks a bone, turtles' shells cannot be fixed with a plaster cast.

One successful treatment that is adopted in many turtle rescue centres around the world is using recycled clasps. Clasps are small metal hooks that are often used to hold together pieces of clothing, like the two straps in a swimming costume.

The crack in the shell is cleaned and then glued together. Clasps are then secured to the shell and thin wire or thread is threaded between them to hold the shell into position. This is kept in place whilst the shell is healing.

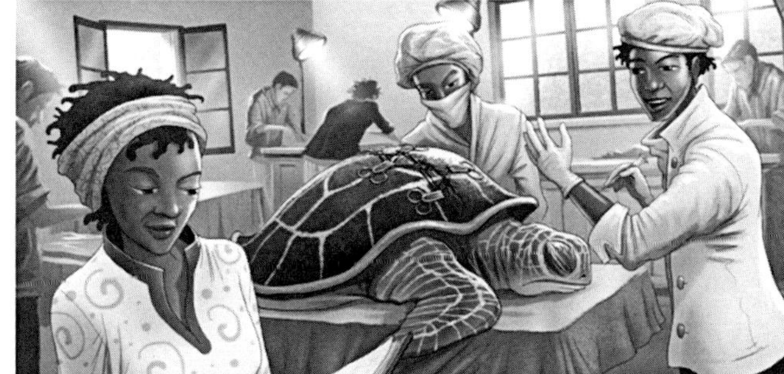

We need your clasps!

This sheet provides the information needed to make a flyer. Ask the pupil to read the text carefully and circle any information they will need to make their flyer. They can then use this information to create the flyer that will encourage people to donate any unwanted metal clasps from their old clothing.

Book 10

Dice game: words with 'ar' spellings

⚀	⚁	⚂	⚃	⚄	⚅
mask	harp	calf	laugh	staff	heart
sharp	blast	palm	alarm	lark	aunt
path	gasp	march	calm	nasty	task
half	ask	charm	calf	art	chart
raft	carpet	spark	far	past	smart

This game is for two players. Each player needs a batch of counters of one colour. The players take turns to throw the die. They read a word in the column that corresponds to the number on the die and place their counter on that word. The first to have three of his/her counters in a row in any direction is the winner.

This sheet may be photocopied by the purchaser. © Phonic Books Ltd 2019

Book 10

Spelling assessment for words with 'ar' spellings

1.

ar	**a**	**al**	**ear**	**au**
car	ask	half	heart	laugh
farm	past	palm	hearth	laughed
spark	blast	calf		

2.

ar	**a**	**al**	**ear**	**au**
startle	rather	almond	hearty	laughter
garden	faster	halves	heartless	
charming	nasty	calmly		

These lists can be used as a spelling assessment at the end of each book. The teacher can add words from list 2 for pupils who are ready for that stage. When dictating a word, first say the word on its own. Next, say a sentence with the word in it (to put the word in the context of a sentence) and then repeat the word. This ensures that the pupil has heard the word correctly, e.g. "Garden. The snail was under a pot in the garden. Garden."